EMPOWERED TO WIN!

4TH ANTHOLOGY EDITION

ALLISON G. DANIELS

AGD PUBLISHING SERVICES, LLC

TABLE OF CONTENTS

INTRODUCTION
Allison G. Daniels

Empowered to Win!

Within this *Empowered to WIN* book, each author will walk you through their life experiences and journey of hope and survival in midst of it all. In this Book, the authors will share their testimony to the faith that they stood on to bombard Heaven to make a change in their lives, and, also, you will see how they never gave up because they trusted and believed in God. Although they dealt with past disappointments, by God's grace they continued to stay connected to the call and purpose God had for their lives.

Empowered to Win!

In this book, *Empowered to WIN*, your journey of wholeness will begin with the power, the praise, and the presence of the Lord. This Book will challenge you to take back your life and enable you to walk in your authority so that you can face tomorrow --today.

RECLAIM YOUR IDENTITY AND PROCEED TO WIN
Dr. Betsy Evans-Bennett

ABOUT THE AUTHOR

Dr. Betsy Evans-Bennett is a highly sought-after Keynote Speaker, International Best Selling Author, Mentor, Certified Christian/Life and Business Coach and a leading authority on Women's Empowerment. Dr. Betsy works with groups, individuals, and organizations to amplify their authority and empower them to become their best selves.

Contact Dr. Evans-Bennett:

- Email- bennettbetsy26@yahoo.com

- Facebook-Bernalee Spice

- Instagram -bernalee_31

CHAPTER 1

RECLAIM YOUR IDENTITY AND PROCEED TO WIN

"She silently stepped out of the race she never wanted to be in found her lane and proceeded to win." ~**Unknown**

Hey! Psssst! Yes, you. Are you allowing fear of the unknown to keep you stuck? Have you ever felt lost, abandoned, or simply in a state of bewilderment? Have you ever felt as though you lack purpose and life isn't waiting for you but passing you by? Have you ever felt like a complete failure, or has anyone ever told you that you will never amount to anything? How about feeling like life has consistently dealt you bad hands no matter how often you reshuffled the deck?

That used to be me. I was that chick. I questioned God at every turn. Lord why am I going through all this? When will it all come to an end? I remembered my days that turned into nights reciting Psalms 37 and 91 and asking God PUH-LEEEEEEEZE do not let my enemies laugh at me. I was broken, overwhelmed and tired of it all. What I didn't realize is that I was living in a self-defeated mindset. A stinking-think-

3

ing mindset. A fearful mindset. I just wanted to die to avoid having to think about life's woes. Throwing in the towel seemed like the best option.

One day as I painfully and teary-eyed began questioning God, a thought came to me and spoke life into my entire being and awoke every dead cell. I thought to myself that like Esther I was made for such a time as this and that I will not die but live and declare the works of the Lord. It was then that I knew I had to reclaim my identity in Christ and empower my win!

2 Timothy 1:7 (KJV) says: "For God has not given us the spirit of fear but of power and of love and of a sound mind." As a staunch believer of God's words, I took it literally and used it to fashion a victorious mindset. Was it easy? No, but I insisted on keeping in memory that life isn't canceled so in spite of the pain, fear and worry I had to forge ahead. I had to push past the pain. Like a board game, there are rules, objectives and a million ways to win, but the first and foremost rule is to "make a move."

Napoleon Hill says: "Life is a game board. Time is your opponent. If you procrastinate you will lose the game. You must make a move to be victorious." But wait, hold on a second! Was I ready to challenge myself out of my comfort zone? Hhhhmmm Laaaawd this was going to be a hard nut to crack, but life they say begins at the edge of your comfort zone. I had to snatch my power back. So, I girded my loins with discipline, dedication, determination, and faith and kept a mental note that I am destined to win. With this new mindset, I implemented strategies that would ensure my victory.

1. I dismissed the mindset of doom and gloom, failure and negativity and cultivated a mindset of trial and error that will lead to success. We do not manifest what we want, rather we manifest what we believe. If you believe it, then you will achieve it. Our thoughts shape who we are and what we become. Winning starts with the thought that you are a winner.

2. I declared and decreed victory over my life, knowing and believing that there is power in the tongue. The Bible says in Proverbs 18:21 that life and death is in the power of the tongue. I spoke life.

3. I changed the narrative from self-defeating to self-serving. I had to witness the manifestation of God's words in my life. I thought about how Jesus defeated the cross, death and the grave and how privileged I was to walk in that same victory.

4. I took bold steps. I decided to risk it all or nothing. I had to give life all I had. After all I was afforded the opportunity to live. Fear is nothing but an illusion and it would not restrict or confine me instead I would allow faith to catapult me into my destiny.

5. I stepped out of my comfort zone, realizing that it was a beau-

tiful place to be in but nothing good ever happens there. I had to be bold and brave enough to break down barriers and shatter glass ceilings. Truth is you may make mistakes, face difficult choices, fail once or twice but you will never know what awaits on the other side if you don't step out of that comfort zone.

6. I did it afraid. I hightailed my plans into action and went full speed ahead. I made the move. The most difficult step is always the first step. I broke up with fear engaged faith and found the courage required to conquer anything that tried to prevent me from living out loud.

7. I engulfed myself with like-mindedness with people who supported my vision and aspired to win also.

I was now buckled up and ready for an exciting ride through life's twists and turns, and life's ups and downs. Guess what? Life happens but God will always provide an escape. Wake up every morning and reaffirm yourself. Here are a few affirmations I've used along the way:

- I am bent but not broken.

- I am an overcomer.

- I am in control.

- I am strong.

- I am destined to win.

Your current situation is never your final destination. Do not discount your future because of where you are today. Find what makes you happy and pursue it. Define success for yourself. Set attainable goals and develop strategies to meet them. Play to your strengths and keep your expectations high. God is a promise keeper, He will fulfill His promises to you. Do not quit on yourself (quitting for me was never an option). Align your actions with your purpose. Choose to be your best coach and cheerleader. Keep your self-talk positive. To get to this victorious point in my life took guts, faith in God and rock-bottom strength. Life is a process, learn from it, grow and glow through it. You are your limitation, take the limits off and soar.

I will leave you with Philippians 1:6 "Being confident of this very thing that He who has begun a good work in you will perform it until the day of Jesus Christ."

Love, light, peace, and blessings!

Winning in Your Finances
Bernadette M. Brawner

About the Author

Bernadette M. Brawner is the Founder and CEO of BB Coaching and Consulting and the Founder and Director of Sisters Helping Empower Each Other (SHEE). Bernadette is a shining example of resilience and determination. Her journey from adversity to success in both personal and professional spheres showcases the power of perseverance. As a

Certified Life Coach with an MBA background, Bernadette empowers clients to transform their lives and strategic direction. Bernadette is a Certified Life Coach, an accomplished author, and motivational speaker. She inspires women through her faith-driven publications and co-authored anthologies. Ms. Brawner is a native DC Washingtonian and a mother of one adult daughter, Makeala.

Contact Bernadette:

- **Email**: bernadette@bernadette-brawner.com

- **Website**: https://bernadettebrawner.com

- **Facebook**: @BBCoachingandConsultingLLC

- **IG**: @BernadetteBrawnerconsulting

- **Contact number**: 301-538-2207

CHAPTER 2

Winning in Your Finances: Cultivating Strong Relationships for Financial Victory

What is your relationship with money, healthy or unhealthy? Are you financially fit or do you need a tune-up? No matter where you are in your financial health, there is always room for improvement. Just as we evaluate things that we purchase or are being evaluated on our jobs or clients. We must take the time to review our progress. The same goes for evaluating our financial portfolio. There are countless businesses that can assist you with this task. You do not have to walk this journey alone.

Winning in your finances to obtain financial victory demonstrates the impact personal relationships, financial literacy, and life triggers have on our financial perspectives. I would like to emphasize the critical nature of our relationship with money, which is shaped by our upbringing and teachings, or lack thereof, during childhood plays a major role in how we view money. To achieve financial success requires one to be intentional as well as cultivating a lifestyle that leads to debt-free living and financial freedom. Furthermore, fostering healthy relationships with others is just as vital as our relationship with money as well as the need for personal stability and well-being in our pursuit of financial victory.

When our relationships are healthy, every aspect of our lives thrives. How many of us want to be successful? Yes, all of us, but we must put the work in to get to a level where we focus more on financial stability and not focus on being like someone who appears to be living the life and making a salary that can afford our needs and wants. We must be careful not to compare our lives with others. A lot of people are not being honest about their way of living, but social media paints a picture that some are living a dream life. Let's take a closer look at the gardening process and draw inferences on our relationship with people and money.

I would like to use an analogy between relationships and a gardener's planting process. Connections to self, others, and money are akin to planting flowers. Relationships allow us to sow seeds, nurture growth, provide nourishment, and flourish in various facets of life. Building and sustaining relationships requires three straightforward steps, acknowledging that although they may seem simple, they require effort. In this analogy gardening expertise is not a must, however I encourage you to reflect on the process of gardening and compare it to the cultivation of relationships. Like plants requiring soil, sunlight, water, and protection from weeds to thrive, relationships also demand specific elements for growth. The necessities for relationship growth are:

Soil: Just as plants need rich soil as a foundation for life, our relationships require nutrients such as peace, love, encouragement, and wisdom. These serve as the foundation for healthy connections, in Ephesians 3:17 tells us that we are to be rooted and grounded in the Love of Christ. Just as the plant needs nutrients from rich soil to thrive, so do our relationships. Our nutrients are peace, love, encouragement, and wisdom.

Sunlight: Plants need sunlight to grow, and we need the energy and positive influences from others to foster healthy relationships. Sunlight manifests in various forms, including smiles, helping hands, forgiveness, laughter, education, time investment, integrity, grit, and sisterhood, among others.

Water: Just like plants need water to stay alive, our relationships require fellowship with others and fellow believers. Recognizing that God did not intend for us to grow alone, we must seek connection and encouragement from one another. You see, 1 Thessalonians 5:11 tells us, "Therefore encourage one another and build one another up, just as you are doing. Water is the vessel for the nutrients we need to grow.

How many of you know that real relationships are indispensable in our lives, and it cautions against neglecting the presence of "weeds" in relationships? Weeds come in various forms, such as toxic friendships, bitterness, anger, love of money, overspending, and increasing debt. Like how weeds choke plants, hindering growth and creating an unfavorable atmosphere, weeds in relationships distract us and can easily crush weaker connections. However, strengthening ourselves with good soil, sunlight, and refreshing water empowers us to win and be successful in life. By doing so, we deepen our financial foundations and nurture relationships with people and money, allowing them to flourish.

I would like to share a personal story about the lack of financial education when I was a youth and the societal taboo surrounding money conversations. This experience became a trigger for me as I became an adult, which caused me to distance myself from financial literacy. However, through the influence of individuals who valued their finances, I gradually had a mindset shift and became immersed in financial concepts, studying the subject, and paying close attention to my financial triggers which led to tendencies to overspend. I recognized the importance of knowing and addressing these triggers, ensured that I was familiar with my own financial behaviors. All the forementioned are essential for successful financial management.

I would conclude with a "call to action," by providing a set of principles to live by for achieving victory in personal finances. These principles include paying tithes, shifting mindset regarding money, taking charge of finances without fear, forgiving oneself for past financial neglect, pursuing personal finance courses, understanding monthly income and expenses, creating a budget or financial plan, paying off credit card debt and loans, saving six months of expenses for emergencies, investing in stocks, bonds, and life insurance, reading books on financial teracy, and starting over and returning to the budgeting process if one oes off track. Above all, I would like to emphasize the importance of ticking to the financial plan and taking immediate action.

n conclusion, be empowered by taking control of your finances. The ime is now, why? Because *your finances matter*. There is great power in ultivating strong relationships and acquiring financial knowledge to chieve long-term financial success. I encourage you to incorporate the teps mentioned to overcome financial challenges and prioritize their inancial well-being.

"The journey of a thousand miles, begins with a single step." – *Lao-Tzu*

Unscathed but Not Unchanged
CC Channell

About the Author

CC Channell has a genuine passion to serve others, which continues to flourish through a rewarding career in human resources. As a Training Manager and newly certified Life Coach, she loves to design empowerment tools and conduct presentations to equip individuals and groups in the areas of leadership development as well as personal, professional, and spiritual growth. In her first book, *The Sowing Kit: Reflection from Tears to Joy*, her captivating poetry, stories, and testimony of victory through challenges express just how much she loves the Lord and loves to inspire others to fight the good fight of faith.

CC is a native New Yorker, now residing in South Carolina, where she also enjoys volunteer assignments in a variety of community organizations.

Visit www.ksginspirations.com to learn more.

CHAPTER 3

UNSCATHED BUT NOT UNCHANGED

"Blessed is he whose transgression is forgiven, whose sin is covered. Blessed is the man to whom the Lord does not impute iniquity." –

Psalm 32:1-2

I was distraught because of emotional abandonment but my God kept me.

I was offended because of accusations of poor parenting but my Father taught me.

I became stronger because my God molded me through those sleepless midnight hours.

I became wiser because my God's Word renewed my mind.

I can smile because my God caught every tear and watered my dry, weary bones back to health.

I can sing because the Spirit heard my cries and turned them into songs of praise.

I can love because my God loved me through my sin, shortcomings and emotional battles.

I can forgive because my God gave me chance after chance to try again each day.

I can hope because my God is faithful and has a plan for me.

I am unscathed but not unchanged because I am transformed.

I am made new ...all things become new by His mercy and grace.

This testimony could have only happened with God's healing, so I pray that this encourages you. To be unscathed is defined as without suffering any injury, damage, or harm. Unchanged means remaining the same, unaltered, not changed. As I reflect on a specific segment of my journey as a mother and wife, I am unscathed but not unchanged. Although I am a people-person, and it's my nature to care deeply for others and help when I can, not every and anyone gets the same level of energy from me. However, probably just like yours to you, my family matters more than the world to me. Warning: that's where the enemy will work double-time to seek, kill, and destroy. For generations past and to come, his one stone of discourse is thrown to take out all birds at one time.

I was in a committed friendship-to-marriage for over fifteen years, which simultaneously began to grow during the crucial years of raising children. I would be lying if I said that everything was always great because it wasn't, but what was great about us is that it was always real – and that's what I loved. Becoming a blended family was new for all of us, and we got along well -love was there through thick and thin- for years, which is why we got married. There are so many happy memories of laughter, family trips, jokes, and pranks in the house. I would say they may even outweigh the dark times. This is not about shaming or blaming any one of us for all that happened. This was written when I realized that despite any of the pain, discord, sadness, and frustration experienced, there were important lessons to be gained from growing through the fallouts, making honest mistakes in things said or done, getting through the "never-seen-this-before" mishaps and respecting differences. Raising children requires strength, patience, and fortitude. Many decisions I made as a single parent were based on establishing and maintaining a loving, peace-filled, and stable home. I believe that as Mom, my role didn't and will never require perfection but rather genuineness. I learned early on that I had to be real in my relationship with Jesus, living an active faith that my children could glean from as they grew and ventured onto their individual paths. It's still important to me that my children (young adults) see my testimony is to fight the good fight of faith come what may. Marriage also requires strength, patience, and fortitude, as well as vulnerability, humility, and staying power. As a wife, there was so much to learn about myself and him. I loved the laughter in our friendship. I loved the trust and loyalty. As uncomfortable as it was at times, I even loved the challenges in learning how to communicate. We had to learn how to talk about everything such as likes and dislikes, finances, coordinating schedules, parenting styles, and praying and reading Scripture together. I didn't know exactly how to do these things, partly because of shyness, but there was no one else with whom I wanted to experience this than him. Why? Because your home is to be a safe haven.

We all need that safe place to retreat and a soft spot to land when life does what it does. Life is unpredictable, people are unpredictable – and we're all on this journey to learn as we live. Well, the marriage didn't last but there's still a friendship, and our children have stepped into early adulthood. I admit that we obviously neglected to let love rule while learning to live through the experiences. Nothing good comes easy so it takes each family member to stay committed to do the work and build your team! God is the Coach and He makes the calls. He never cancels you.

As a woman, I thank God that I am unscathed but not unchanged by that segment of my journey.

Today, I thank God that my hurts have healed, and I don't feel the sting of bitterness. Though I experienced rejection, I said goodbye to the damage of brokenness. I am not walking in a state of suffering because I have been restored to wholeness. My purpose did not end when my parenting style transitioned from raising children to cheering for my MVPs. I have hope and joy because my future is bright. I encourage you to seek truth, peace, and growth through the challenges that life is presenting to you. Don't get blinded by the discourse. I learned that forgiveness is the key to restoration of joy and love for self and others. It takes a relentless determination and grace to receive forgiveness and to extend it – and you really shouldn't try to do one without the other. Forgive and live.

Questions for Reflection

1. Do you want to be healed?

2. What steps are you willing to take to seek wise counsel for your emotional, spiritual, financial, and physical healing?

3. How have you come to understand the power of forgiveness?

I'm Standing Strong on the Promises of God
Evangelist Tamala Coleman

ABOUT THE AUTHOR

Evangelist Tamala Jenise Coleman is a 7X best-selling author with 14 published books.

Tamala has been writing for over 16 years and she has developed the potential to write, intentionally, to encourage and inspire others. Also,

Tamala has her credits as a director and producer of stage plays and film. To date, Tamala has won several film-script credits. Tamala is also the Founder and Editor & Chief of NSpire Christian Magazine. Tamala strives to empower women and inspire the masses with the power of faith.

Tamala is also a member of "Women with Wings, International" where she is on the Board of Directors. This foundation is Christian-based and assists women who have been entrapped in domestic violence and sex-trafficking. She has also hosted a number of podcasts for 6 years, including "Spiritually Speaking" on AMFM247 Broadcasting Radio Show, and "Amazing Grace" on TalkZone Radio where she interviews ministers, authors, business owners, and just everyday people with a testimony to share with the world and share the Good News of Jesus Christ. Tamala is currently the host of "The Outpouring Podcast Show" weekly on Wednesday nights.

Tamala is the recipient of several awards: Radio Personality of the Year (ACHI Magazine Awards 2019); "Women Rocking the Web Awards' 2022; Writer's Magazine Cover Page Feature; ATL Magazine; 2022 Recipient of the Business Owner of the Year ACHI Awards and 2023 Playwright of the Year for the NSpire Image Awards. She has received many more accomplishments and accolades, which are too many to name herein.

Tamala worships devotedly with New Springfield Missionary Baptist Church for over 40 years and she serves as a Sunday School Teacher & Minister.

Tamala is a loving and devoted wife to Brian Coleman and mother to their three wonderful children, Thaddeus, Tiffanie, and Brianna.

Contact Evangelist Coleman:

- www.nspirechristianmagazine.com

- www.tamalacolemanbooks@yolasite.com

- Facebook: Tamala Coleman

- Instagram: Iam_tamalacoleman

- Email: tcpraise14@gmail.com

CHAPTER 4

I'M STANDING STRONG ON THE PROMISES OF GOD

"Therefore, whoever hears these sayings of Mine, and does them, I will liken him to a wise man who built his house on the rock: and the rain descended, the floods came, and the winds blew and beat on that house; and it did not fall, for it was founded on the rock." – **Matthew 7:24-24**

In the above Scripture, Jesus tells us of the wise man who chose to build his house on the rock –rock solid, steady, and true foundation. He could have chosen a more convenient foundation that would crumble under pressure, or be moved by the wind, but he chose a strong foundation that would not waver in a storm. Just like this wise man, you must take care to build your life on the true, unshakable foundation! The English Dictionary's definition of unshakable means someone's trust or belief is unshakable, it is firm and cannot be made weaker or destroyed: She was blessed with an unshakable belief in her own abilities; to not be weakened. I have learned that the Word of God is the only foundation that will never fail, change, or pass away. Many people spend so much of their lives waiting for happiness or waiting for retirement years to find out that they are empty and unfulfilled.

Ephesians 2:10 says, "For we are His workmanship, created in Christ Jesus for good works, which God prepared beforehand that we should walk in them." God has prepared good works for us to accomplish! He has a plan for each one of us that requires so much more than the simple pursuit of pleasure, and when we choose to build our house on the Rock and Foundation of God; we will have righteousness, peace, and joy in the Kingdom of God. Put God First!

Many believers are of the mindset that they need only to be good enough, kind enough, or spiritual enough to be right with God. Some may even think they are saved simply because they believe God exists. But you can only be made right with Him through Jesus who is the way, the truth, and the life. In John 14, Jesus tells us that no one can come to the Father except through Him. We also need to understand that God cares so deeply for us that He wants to be a part of our daily lives. He does not want us to *hope* that we are behaving well enough or doing enough good deeds to make up for our mistakes. As He shows us in His Word, the only way to be made righteous is through faith in Jesus.

Faith grows upon a solid foundation. God loves us just the way we are, but He does not and He will not leave us the way we are; our faith is meant to grow and become stronger throughout our life's journey, especially the Christian journey.

In 2 Thessalonians 1:3 Paul writes, "We ought always to thank God for you, brothers and sisters, and rightly so, because your faith is growing more and more, and the love all of you have for one another is increasing." (NIV). We are not designed to only exist on a foundation, but to continuously build upon our faith as we walk with God. As we grow on this journey, we must remain steadfast and unmovable. In my life I have endured much, and I have overcome much, and I must say, that if it had not been for my faith in God, I would have given up a long time ago. I am sure I am not alone; many of us are walking on grounds that eventually would have swallowed us up or we may have fallen deep into an abyss, but due to our faith, we are still standing and walking on a strong foundation of God's Word and His promises.

There is a song that I love very much, and it states:

I'm still standing,

I'm still trusting

I'm still holding on to what I believe

Still motivated

Fully persuaded

I'm still standing

Standing on the Word

On the Word that's in my heart.

Your Word says I am healed

So that means I am healed

Your Word says I am free

So that means I am free

Your Word says I am

More than a conqueror

Through Jesus

Standing, standing

Standing on the promises

Of Christ my Savior

Standing, standing

Standing on the promises of God.

These words state just how we should stand in our faith, and we must have an unshakable faith, that even when things around us are falling to pieces. I can say and I declare that I am still standing on the Word that holds me; the Word that heals me, the Word that frees me and the Word that has kept me through it all.

I'm STILL STANDING and TRUSTING in God and standing on His promises!

You may be going through trying times right now, or maybe you feel like you are at a stand-still in your life and you just don't know how you are going to make it. Yes, God has a word for you –for your soul. You are an overcomer and I encourage you to hold on to your faith. Pray and seek God. No matter how hard it gets, hold on to unshakable faith. I am reminded of the familiar Scripture in Hebrews 11, "Now faith is the substance of things hoped for, the evidence of things not seen." Throughout my life as a believer, I have come to depend on this Scripture as an encouragement. Why? Because throughout my life I had to realize that without faith I have nothing; without my faith I am nothing. Honestly, I would have lost my mind. Yet, God has kept me through my many tests and trials, challenges, and tribulations. As a podcast host for the past three years I have had the opportunity to speak with both women and men who were guests on my shows and many shared their life's journey with me –the good, the bad, and the ugly, and as I listened to their sharing, I had to count my blessings because I felt that my life was worthless and that I had endured some things that I never shared with anyone ,yet perfect strangers unapolo-getically shared their intense life stories with me and the world through my podcast.

So I am sharing this testimony with you, because many of us are not true to ourselves, because the reality is that we all have a testimony and we all have a past. Your experiences may not be my experiences, your testimony is not my testimony, however, we all have testimonies, and they are not just for us, but for others who need to know that they too can have this unshakable faith and they too can stand, even in the midst of their situation. This unshakable faith to stand, even in the hardest times, can seem lonely sometimes; it can even feel exhausting, especially if you are trying to stand on the Word of God.

Hebrews 11:16 states "But now they desire a better, that is, a heavenly country. Therefore, God is not ashamed to be called their God, for He has prepared a city for them." Faith is the substance or the guarantee that those things which you are waiting for will come to pass. Faith is the evidence we can have when we cannot see the manifestation. Faith begins when you drown your doubts, cast off fear and anchor in the Truth of God's Word. God is a rewarder of those who diligently seek Him. If you believe that you are not experiencing His grace or the deliverance you need, seek Him. I refuse to allow anyone, or anything to stand between me and faith and my trust in God. So, as you read these words, I pray that you too will stand on your faith. Stand, therefore! Stand and know that God will never leave you nor forsake you.

In Ephesians 6:13-17, it says "Therefore take up the whole armor of God, that you may be able to withstand in the evil day, and having done all, to stand. Stand therefore, having girded your waist with truth, having put on the breastplate of righteousness, and having shod your

feet with the preparation of the gospel of peace; above all, taking th
shield of faith with which you will be able to quench all the fiery dart
of the wicked one. And take the helmet of salvation, and the sword o
the Spirit, which is the word of God;"

It takes faith and God's grace to follow God's plan for our lives. Goc
is the Author and the Finisher of our faith. Taking the chance to ste￼
out of your comfort zone and walk in faith, is what it is all about
that's where the miracle happens because moving in the direction o
uncharted waters in your life can be very scary, but praying to Goc
helps to establish that relationship with Him and as you grow in Him
as you delight yourself in Him, He will give you the desires of you￼
heart. We must understand that faith always means risk. Everything ir
life is a risk.

Ecclesiastes 10:8 says, "He who digs a pit will fall into it, And whoever
breaks through a wall will be bitten by a serpent. He who quarries
stones may be hurt by them, And he who splits wood may be endan￼
gered by it." There's nothing we can do that doesn't have some element
of risks or taking chances, if you will, in or with it. But the greatest risk
of all is how we relate to other people and how we relate to God to risk
in doing something about those relationships.

Mark 12:30 says, "And you shall love the Lord your God with all your
heart, with all your soul, with all your mind, and with all your strength.'
This is the first commandment." You take a risk when you love with
all your heart. Is it worth it? Absolutely. Especially loving God with al￼

our heart. When I think about my husband and how I love him and he loves me, we both took risks in a new relationship, not knowing if it would work or not. Yet, after 17 years I can truly say it was worth it. We would not have known it if I had not taken the risk.

Jesus reminded us that one of the greatest mistakes we can make is to play it safe with our lives. He said, "If you try to keep your life for yourself, you'll lose it." True scripture! Faith is stepping out and doing what God has asked you to do when you can't see what will happen in the end.

You don't know exactly what God is going to do in the end, but you know He's asking you to step out in faith. I can remember when I finally made the decision to write my first book; I realized I couldn't keep talking the good talk –that I was going to do it; I had to make a move towards writing the book. I had to pick up a pen and write something down; I had to start the book.

Talk is cheap until you make a move. So, I encourage you to step out in faith; lean on God's unchanging hand and believe God for that unshakable faith, and, oh, keep standing!

PRAYER

Heavenly Father, teach us to lean on Your Word and trust Your Word. God, give us Your strength to hold on, even in trying circumstances and difficult times. Help us God to stand always on Your promises and have the unshakable faith that only You alone can give. We trust You and we give You all the honor, the praise and the glory, in Jesus' name Amen!

Winning in My Purpose
Damona Daniels

About the Author

Damona Daniels is an International Best-Selling Author and Speaker. She wrote and published her first book at the age of 6 years old. Her book is entitled, *Bully Me No More* as well as a workbook.

She is the contributing author of the book series, *Empowered to Win 2nd Edition*, and *Empowered to Win, 4th Edition*. She currently teaches choreography (cheerleading) at James Madison Middle School and choreographs dances for VYBE dance studio.

A graduate and 2023 Class President of Frederick Douglass High School, she spoke at her graduation. She is the social media Director of AGD Publishing Services, LLC. She is a Legacy Speaker at the 2023 Women Empowered to Win Summit. She loves to dance and travel. Her goal is to graduate from college and own her own dancing studio to help underprivilege children. She is currently pursuing her nursing degree with a concentration in theatrical dancing at Bowie State University.

CHAPTER 5

WINNING IN MY PURPOSE

"For I know the plans I have for you, declares the Lord, plans for welfare and not for evil, to give you a future and a hope." Jeremiah 29:11 KJV

Winning in my purpose required me to stay focused. It required me to focus on my goals for college. When I looked up the word purpose, Webster's dictionary stated what purpose was.

It means something that one hopes or intends to accomplish.

Winning in my purpose is me doing what I believe God has called me to do. I learned at an early age how to stay focused on a set goal. I learned at an early age how to set goals and then what I needed to do to achieve them.

My sister and I learned the four rules that our parents set on how to achieve our goals. Here are the four goals that we were taught in our household, and I am sharing them now.

1. Write the vision down.

2. Gain clarity on it meaning research.

3. Decide how you want to proceed.

4. And then act on it.

Although I was young, I knew that I had to continue to believe in myself and I would one day achieve my goals. My confidence and self-esteem were nurtured at home which is my foundation for my future.

Winning in my purpose requires me to aim higher, to reach for a set target on what I what to do in life, to pursue my dreams, to stay on the right path and be intentional about making a difference making an impact. One of the two of my dreams and goals in life is to become a famous hip hop and modern dancer and to own my own dancing studio to help teach the under privilege how to be creative and start their own business.

I love this quote by a mentor that I look up to

Mrs. Debbie Allen and her quote reads

"But out of limitations comes creativity."

My second dream and goal is to complete college and earn my degree in Nursing to assist the elderly and make a difference and an impact. I believe that God has a great plan so I'm walking in what I think God is calling me to do. I never thought that I would write a book because

I did not believe that that was my calling, but I wrote a book at the tender age of 6 years old with AGD Publishing Services and my plan is to revise it and make a difference with our youth.

Winning in my purpose requires me to focus on my set goals in life. To be true to myself as I journey on my assignments. Never let the things that didn't happen in life stop you from moving forward. I learned that I have what it takes down on the inside of me to make a difference. Life is a journey and I'm going to achieve what I have set out to do for myself. I believe that I can make a difference and help others along the way.

I have been teaching the youth how to dance and creating their dance steps since the age of fourteen. As the class president of my high school graduating class of 2023, I planned out events, parties, and community events. I have been working with the youth now since graduating from high school and I will continue to give of my time and service to empower my youth to be the best that they can be.

I believe that winning in my purpose is my new charge for 2023, for me to follow my dreams and execute them, accomplish them, and achieve them.

Winning in my purpose is:

    1. Pursue my dreams.

    2. Act on it and make it happen.

3. Build a platform for others to advance in their dreams.

4. Step into my purpose and make it work for me.

BREAKTHROUGH TO YOUR DREAMS
Pastor Felicia Edmond

ABOUT THE AUTHOR

Pastor Felicia Edmond is an Amazon international best-selling author, minister, and podcast host. Pastor Felicia has a passion for seeing people encounter breakthroughs and freedom in areas where they are challenged and receive the love of God. She lives by the fact that God has created us uniquely, and we can discover our God-given purpose as we seek Him.

Pastor Felicia is the author of *Breakthrough Book of Poems and Prayers* and the *Arise Devotional Book*. She is also a contributing author in the following anthologies with Visionary Author Reverend Allison G Daniels: *Empowered to Win:2nd Edition, Empowered to Win:3rd Edition*, and *Women Be Free*.

Pastor Felicia is a workshop speaker regarding emotional healing in overcoming depression and rejection. She has served in various ministry capacities through counseling, mentoring, teaching, and preaching. Pastor Felicia, along with her husband, are in the process of launching Grace and Faith Christian Church in Maryland, teaching the love, grace, and freedom of God. She obtained a Bachelor of Science in Accounting from Hampton University and a Master of Counseling from Trinity University. She is married to her husband, Pastor Jerry, and they have two beautiful children, Joelle, and Jonathan.

CHAPTER 6

BREAKTHROUGH TO YOUR DREAMS

"For we are God's handiwork, created in Christ Jesus to do good works, which God prepared in advance for us to do" Ephesians 2:10

The Lord has placed many dreams in my heart, and I had to learn to take them seriously. God keeps his promises and has great plans for our lives. Jeremiah 29:11 states for I know the thoughts that I think toward you says the Lord, thoughts of peace and not of evil, to give you a future and a hope. God showed me portions of His plans for me as a young adult. He showed me that I would be a counselor, a minister speaking at conferences and workshops on depression and purpose, and He later showed me that my husband and I would become Pastors. When my husband and I were courting, God showed me that we would be in ministry and people would know us by our expression of God's love. There were many seasons in our lives where my circumstances did not line up with what God placed on my heart. After many years of homeschooling my children, serving in various church ministry capacities, and overcoming depression, suicidal thoughts, and family challenges, I realized these dreams were still in my heart. Philippians 1:6 states that being confident of this very thing, that He who has begun a

ALLISON G. DANIELS

good work in you will complete *it* until the day of Jesus Christ. God is faithful to fulfill His purpose in our lives no matter how dark it seems. I had to receive God's healing, allow God to select the ministry circle He ordained for my life, and take the first step, no matter how minor it seems, because I could not let my dreams die. I could breakthrough to my dreams.

Embrace God's Healing

God is truly my Healer. I encountered trauma in my past and needed healing at my core. I encountered depression and suicidal thoughts because I could not see my worth because of what people spoke into my life through the years, and I internalized those thoughts. They spoke words of failure and despair. I felt like I was not enough and could not succeed based on feelings of rejection and disappointment. This attack was the enemy trying to stop my destiny. I could not embrace my destiny without God's healing. Healing is a process. I began fully embracing the healing through God's Word, understanding God's love, and forgiving myself and others. Ephesians 3:17-19 states that Christ may dwell in your hearts through faith; that you, being rooted and grounded in love, may be able to comprehend with all the saints what *is* the width and length and depth and height to know the love of Christ which passes knowledge; that you may be filled with all the fullness of God. I began to embrace the love of the King of Kings and realized that I was the King's daughter. My worth came from Jesus dying for me. I had to really meditate on that fact and really internalize it. As I understood God's love and embrace, He could show me my destiny again. I wanted to live and not die and declare the works of the Lord. He would not let those dreams die and I could breakthrough to obtain my dreams.

God Ordained Ministry Support

God had to change my inner circle regarding ministry to take me to the next level. God placed me around people who were excited about what I brought to the table as I was excited for them. Previously, I was with people who placed me in a box and could not see my potential. They would say, "I do not see you doing that," or "did God really tell you that you could accomplish that ministry endeavor? I can only see a particular individual accomplishing this task and not you." Wonderfully, God slowly began to place me around people of purpose. We were like-minded and encouraged one another in ministry. We began to tell each other with God all things are possible, and you can birth your purpose. It is difficult to fully embrace your destiny if the enemy consistently uses the people around you as naysayers. You will spend an enormous time fighting the enemy's words rather than building your purpose. It becomes a distraction, which is why Philippians 2:2-8 states, "Fulfill my joy by being like-minded, having the same love, *being* of one accord of one mind. *Let* nothing *be done* through selfish ambition or conceit, but in lowliness of mind, let each esteem others better than himself. Let each of you look out not only for his own interests but also for the interests of others." We can love and uplift one another for God's glory and bring people into the Kingdom. We need to hear the Holy Spirit telling us whom we should surround ourselves with in our kingdom purposes. It will all be for His glory so that we can stay kingdom-minded and make disciples.

It Does Not Yet Appear

Once I began healing and changing my ministry circle, I took small steps toward my dreams. Do not despise the day of small beginnings. Zechariah 4:10 states, "For who has despised the day of small things? For these seven, rejoice to see a plumb line in the hand of Zerubbabel. They are the eyes of the Lord, which scan to and from throughout the whole earth." My first step was to begin writing poetry about the emotional healing God placed on my heart. As the poems were healing me, I realized that it was also for the healing of others. I became a published author, which led to open doors. Secondly, I had fulfilled my master's degree in counseling before I had my children. However, God showed me that one day I would be a Licensed Clinical Professional Counselor (LCPC), which required a few additional classes before taking the exam. My first step was to contact my university and enroll in the first course. I am well on my way to completing the steps to becoming an LCPC. Third, I began speaking engagements regarding depression and rejection through my broadcast and other virtual workshops and conferences. Finally, my husband and I are preparing to launch the church that God has ordained for us to pastor others showing God's love. I am taking steps toward my purpose, and each step makes a difference. Each step can touch someone's life. God never forgets His promises and purposes. These dreams are being fulfilled many years later, and it is the beginning. Never forget what God showed you, no matter how many years it has been. God created You for a purpose and wants to use You for His glory. I have taken a few steps toward my destiny, and it does not yet appear what will be revealed in me. 1 John 3:2 Beloved, now we are children of God; and it has not yet been revealed what we shall be, but we know that when He is revealed, we shall be like Him, for we shall see Him as He is.

Questions for Reflection

1. What dreams has God placed on your heart, even if they were long ago?

2. Are there hindrances to walking in your destiny? If so, what are those hindrances?

3. Are there areas in your life that need healing? What steps can you take to receive God's love and embrace your healing?

4. What is one step that the Holy Spirit is leading you to take toward your purpose? Please start with your first step.

I AM...
Rev. Tresniece P. Evans

ABOUT THE AUTHOR

Tresniece N. Evans, affectionately known as T, is an accomplished speaker, author, and entrepreneur. Her first book 'Girl Fix Your Crown' became an Amazon best seller.

Tresniece is currently working in the foster care system at a leading government agency. She brings over 20 years of secretarial experience to her field. This coming November she will obtain her Master of Social Work degree from Walden University, then will take this degree and use it to become a licensed therapist focusing on individuals and couples. She will be a trauma-focused therapist and her chosen specialty will be sexual trauma.

In January 2019, she launched her first web series called *Queen Chronicles*, a weekly aired series on Facebook and YouTube where we have "everyday conversations from a Godly Woman's perspective." This past May she launched her podcast entitled '*Living Unapologetically and Bold.*' This is a weekly series that covers all things to inspire women to live in their truth in every area of their lives unapologetically and boldly.

She has presented at various Women's conferences and has conducted workshops and seminars covering topics such as emotional wellness for women, makeup application, and spiritual healing and growth. Tresniece has provided mentoring to many young women on their journey. Recently Tresniece added the title of wife to her resume as she just married the love of her life, Mr. Sherman Evans.

Contact Rev. Evans

- FB Group: Unapologetically & Bold

- IG: Beloved Wholeness Center

EMPOWERED TO WIN!

- Tik Tok: Beloved Wholeness Center

- Email: CoachT@unapologeticallybold.com

CHAPTER 7

I AM...

Before we get into this chapter, there are some questions I want to ask. Who told you that you were not smart enough? Who told you that you would be beautiful if you lost ten more pounds? Who told you that because of your mistakes, you're a failure? Who told you just to be average and not shine? Who told you to be invisible? Who told you that you were worthless? Who told you that you don't matter? Even with all these questions, the biggest question is *why do you or did you believe them?*

When writing this chapter, I was given one purpose, one directive, to remind you of who you are. Yes, you are the one reading this. I want to remind you of how AMAZING you are. When God gave me the chapter title, He intentionally left the final word off because, by the end of this chapter, He wanted you to be able to add your adverb to the end. Maybe it will be *I am bold, or I am confident, or I am fearless, or I am loved, or I am favored*! Each statement is true, but the key is that you believe the statement! In some moments of life, you must remind yourself that you're fearless, but in others, you may have to remind yourself that you are loved.

See, as we say today, "life be lifeing," meaning life has a way of testing everything you know about yourself. Life has a way of making us feel that we are less than Who we are. Broken relationships tend to make us feel like we are unworthy of love. The loss of a career or the rejection of the dream job has a way of making us feel like failures. As great of a tool as social media is, it has created an imaginary perfect world that is impossible to live up to and fostered these feelings of self-doubt. Sometimes things in our past help make up this need to wear a mask and hide who we are. Certain situations in life can crack the very foundation of who we are. Broken relationships, unreleased forgiveness, hurt, anger, grief, depression, unresolved questions all make us question who we are. The most robust believer in God can struggle to believe who God tells them they are. Sis, you are not alone; I struggled to define myself for years. I based my feelings and thoughts of myself on the opinions of others. I was "happy" when it seemed like others accepted me or chose me, but when people's opinions of me changed, so did my feelings about me.

Why were my feelings of self-worth, self-esteem, and confidence all dependent on the opinion of others when the Creator had created me in His perfect image? Why did my "success" depend on others applauding me or telling me how great I am? How did these struggles of "needing" to be accepted impact my ability to live *Unapologetically and Bold*? How was my inability to believe to my core that whatever my I AM....statement was should matter more than what others saw in me? Was my ability to walk, talk, and live in PURPOSE being compromised due to my failure to trust who GOD said I was versus what others thought or said I was?

There was this time when I heard someone say God wants us to be a brand name but that there was a cost to being a brand name. Now before you stop reading this chapter, let me explain. For a moment, think about a brand name that you know. Some brands we know simply by their logo or are known by their name. Some brands are known by the celebrity that has endorsed them. Other brand names are known because they have been around forever. The thing about a brand name is that it's selective about who they want to represent them. How often have you heard or read about a brand that dropped a celebrity because of something they said or did?

The cost of that relationship is not worth the brand's reputation, so they sever ties. For some brands, you never see a discounted special or find them in every store. They are selective about who gets to display their brand. They set their prices to appeal to a particular type of consumer. They are okay with not being sold in every store. Some brands appeal to a specific clientele, and the cost represents them. Yes, these brands may have individuals displaying the knock-off version, but the creator of the brand and the faithful clients know a fake when they see it.

What's my point? So glad you asked...there is a cost associated with becoming a brand. There is a price to pay to be affiliated with specific brands. In other words, having the **CALL** and **ANOINTING** on your life is a cost. Being a brand means you can't be tied to just any relationship. Deciding to be a brand will cost you some stuff. Some connections you refuse to let go of will have to be released. Some of those familiar conversations and actions will have to be changed. Why? Because how you are moving or where your moving is incompatible with the *I AM* brand that God has called you to. Those former things are more compatible with the generic brand or the old you before you read this chapter and book.

There is a level of comfort that comes with being generic. A level of comfort and ease comes with just doing enough to get by. Yes, you pray, but do you do it regularly? Yes, you checked the negative thoughts that entered your mind but only in specific areas because you believe those negative thoughts to be true in other areas. You can become so conditioned to living in a generic way that you accept the generic treatment from others. You accepted that the "one" God promised may sometimes call you back and other times he doesn't. You've accepted that although you want marriage and kids, you have settled for being in "situationalships." You know where he is; your plus one for all events. You know, the one where he has all of the benefits of being your husband benefits but all he wants is to be an intern in your life. You desire more, but because of how you view yourself, you have learned to accept generic behavior from individuals who don't add value to your life. This has led to you being frustrated, hurt and disappointed more times than you count.

Please understand your inability to accept whom God created you to be has allowed open spaces for the enemy to come and attack. Let me explain. When you genuinely love yourself, there are some behaviors you will not put up with. Not believing in what God says to you allows you to settle for the generic in every area of your life. You will settle for incomplete love instead of demanding *total love*. You will choose to do things to fit in instead of being ok with *standing out*. This is the problem with not knowing or accepting your worth-you put yourself in a place to be treated less than who God called you to be.

You didn't pick up the book by chance. You didn't just happen to start reading this book. There is a message that God has been trying to get to you. There is something that God has been wanting to tell you. Sis, you were meant to shine! You were created to be a brand name! There is **Purpose** and **Destiny** attached to your life. God wants you to know that it's time to shift your mindset. It's time to shift your thoughts on how you see yourself. The time is now to choose not to live in the status quo. You must decide that you don't want to be generic anymore. You must decide that I want to live **Unapologetically and Bold** in every area of my life. I want my mindset and life to reflect how God sees me. *NO MORE* trying to blend in, *NO MORE* mumbling your words, *NO MORE* hiding in the shadows, *NO MORE* running from your past, *NO MORE* walking in shame and guilt over your past mistakes. Tell yourself *NO MORE!*

For this to become your reality, you must be willing to shift your mindset and how you **see** yourself, **speak** about yourself, and *believe* what God says about you. You must be willing to allow God to change how you see yourself through His eyes. You must be willing to let the anger and shame go and move past your former mistakes. There was a time when you treated yourself and required those around you to treat you like a brand name. You took special care of yourself, your relationships, and even your relationship with God, but then something rocked you. As a result, your view of yourself shifted, your opinion of God shifted, and your ability to require others to treat you a certain way changed with it. We have all been there, but this chapter and book will remind you that you have been created to be this fabulous and amazing individual! God thought about you before you thought of your parents or even in your mother's womb. God created you! In Jeremiah 1:5 (NIV), God tells you:

"Before I formed you in the womb, I knew you; before you were born, I set you apart; I appointed you as a prophet to the nations."

He goes on to say in Jeremiah 29:11 (NIV)

"For I know the plans I have for you," declares the Lord, "plans to prosper you and not to harm you, plans to give you hope and a future."

Despite all you have ever said or done, God still calls you *BEAUTI-FUL*! He still calls you *CHOSEN*! He still calls you *DAUGHTER*! He still says you're *FAVORED*! He still says you're *ACCEPTED*! He still has **PURPOSE** attached to you! He still calls you **HIS**! He still calls you **ANOINTED**! He still calls you- **BY NAME**!

Listen the moment you start to walk in your new *I Am* _____(you fill in the blank) mindset. Some individuals will not understand it-it's okay. Some may accuse you of thinking you are "all that" - it's okay. By walking in your *I Am* mindset, you are finally in a place where God can show you your value and worth. You get to where you acknowledge that your beauty goes far deeper than what's on the outside. You start to love all of you instead of just pieces of you. Know that even with the abortion, He still calls you everything mentioned above. With the broken marriage, He still calls you all those things above. Even with the rape and molestation, He declares you're all the things mentioned above. Understand that God's selection of you is not based on the surface. Nope, God chose you because of what He placed on the inside of you. And no matter what detours your life has taken, none of it has made you unworthy to be *chosen* and *used* by God. God does not pick us because we are perfect. It's just the opposite of God's selection of us due to our imperfections!

Now that we are at the end of this chapter, do me a favor! Grab a piece of paper. Can I suggest some colorful Post-It notes? Please create some I AM Affirmations. Write down I AM and then add your adverb to it. Post them everywhere you need a reminder of who you are! In your car, at your desk, on your mirror. When the former negative thoughts arise, start saying your I AM Affirmations. When that relationship ends because God has better for you, speak your I AM Affirmations. When life starts lifeing, express your I AM Affirmations. Below are a few to get you started.....As God gives you more, build your list!

I AM BEAUTIFUL! I AM CHOSEN!

I AM the DAUGHTER of a King! I AM FAVORED!

I AM ACCEPTED! I AM PURPOSED!

I AM ANOINTED! I AM FEARLESS!

I AM IMPERFECTLY PERFECT!

Go live today, tomorrow, and every day after Unapologetically and Bold!

THE A-WORD
Sheila Farr

ABOUT THE AUTHOR

Sheila Farr is an eternal optimist! After 20 years of building and managing successful businesses for others, she stepped out and started her own business in 2017. Now, she's the CEO of Gulf Coast Training & Education Services, LLC, in Biloxi, Mississippi, where she helps individuals and small businesses turn struggles into stepping stones by developing personalized business strategies that work.

A multiple-time international best-selling author and publisher, Sheila is a cheerleader for others, writes an inspirational blog called "Thankful and Blessed 365," and is the founder of "Biloxi Reads!," a literacy initiative that serves low-level readers (both children and adults) on the Mississippi Gulf Coast.

She loves to connect with people via her website or on social media sites such as Facebook and LinkedIn.

CHAPTER 8

THE A-WORD

"A stumbling block to the pessimist is a stepping-stone to the optimist." —— Eleanor Roosevelt

Aside from providing an income necessary to meet the basic needs of daily living, work is important because it helps shape our personal identity and gives us a sense of pride and belonging. As humans, we are social beings, so having a community to which we can contribute gives us the feeling that we are making a difference in the lives of others and to the world. It can be difficult to find work that you love to do, but when you are fortunate enough to find it – it is such an incredible blessing.

I spent years searching for just the right job. I worked hard for years in school, earning degree after degree – hoping that one day I would land in a position that would allow me to make a positive impact on the lives of others. Being an eternal optimist, I always sought to leave my workplaces better than I found them. The lover of processes and systems, I made it my silent mission to establish processes in places where there were none, and to develop systems in the most chaotic of places. I usually had fun at work, but from time-to-time in my career,

65

I encountered organizations that had teamwork problems. In these instances, I'd either work to make things better or I'd remove myself from a situation that only brought me frustration from not being in a position to make improvements or changes for the company. I learned much from a series of "bad bosses," and vowed if I were ever in a position to lead others in an organization, that I would definitely do better!

In 2013, I received one of the greatest blessings in my life: a new job as an administrator of a small, independently owned medical practice. Finally, my hard work had paid off and I was in a position that would allow me to do good things and help grow others. I absolutely loved it! For years, I worked with the owner, strategically hiring the best of the best and working hard to make sure we took care of our patients and employees. Before long, we had developed one of the most dynamic teams I'd ever been blessed to lead. The trust factor in our organization was high and our team really cared about the work we were doing – and they cared about each other. We worked hard together, supporting each other daily, and being innovative about our approach to the growth of our business. We were making money, enjoying our work, and having fun doing it all. We were truly blessed! Then suddenly one day, seemingly from out of the blue – our practice owner shared the news that the business had been sold to a corporate entity and that soon, we would all succumb to the A-word: acquisition. I couldn't even speak the word because it had such a negative connotation to it. All of my experience and everything I knew about an acquisition was negative. My heart sank at the realization of what was about to happen, and this feeling permeated my entire body. I was devastated: I felt as though I'd just lost my only child, and I knew that our lives would never be the same. Although there was the promise of no changes to our outstanding organization, I knew that things would never be the same. I'd been through acquisitions before, and this was something I certainly did not want to be part of. The only thing I could think of was all of the bad experiences I'd had before with changeovers in organizations; job losses, pay reductions, and a total upheaval of processes and procedures. I didn't want this for myself, and I surely did not want my team to have to experience any of this. I was shaken to the core!

In the days after the announcement, I made certain to share as much information as I had with our employees. I knew things were about to get shaken up in our world, and I did my best to protect each of my co-workers. Before long, the changes started to happen, and one-by-one, we started to lose many members of our extraordinary team. While the new company did, in fact, work extremely hard to keep some things the same, there are always changes that must be made when companies merge or are acquired, and our situation was no different. As the administrator of the old company, I was responsible for many of the tasks that would be shifted to the new corporation – so there really was no position for me. The new company tried to make one for me, but it was so painful (for them and for me), that they basically just left me there in limbo for a while, trying to keep me on board, but not really knowing what to do with me. Eventually, I asked for a position in marketing. That was something I had a little experience with and was really interested in learning more about, so thankfully, that's where they placed me...on the side and away from the rest of the team. New leadership had to be established, so it was really the best move for all of us...but when I say it was incredibly difficult for me to stand by and watch my beloved company become dismantled, dismembered, and reconfigured – that is really an understatement. It was one of the most painful times in my life. All I knew to do is to pray. I know that when everything in life is changing, our Lord is the one thing that is always constant.

A few years prior to the acquisition, I'd started a small training company as a "side hustle." I love teaching and I love to be busy, so I started helping small businesses and entrepreneurs with business plans and compliance training. I did this in the evenings and on the weekends for several years, but after the acquisition, I found myself being drawn to the idea of starting something new and working independently. That idea became more and more attractive to me, so I began pouring more and more of my free time into my training business; and before long, things had really taken off for me! I went from teaching a few yoga classes weekly and helping one or two friends with their businesses to teaching a wide range of health and wellness courses in our community and assisting international businesses with business planning and strategies. While still maintaining my marketing work for the medical practice, I'd begun to build a successful business as an entrepreneur on he side! This was so exciting to me, because it was something I'd always longed to do and now the Lord had opened the floodgates and was blessing me immensely. It dawned on me one day that I had overcome the negative feelings associated with the loss of my beloved medical practice and was beginning to build something better for myself while walking hand-in-hand with the Lord. This was so exciting to me!

What I learned is that you really want to reinvent yourself in times of adversity, one of the best ways I've found to do that is simply to be true to who you are. When you're walking – and working - in your purpose according to the gifts that the Lord has given you – and in the way that He has called you to do it – you cannot fail. When an acquisition rocked my world and sent me into an ocean of uncertainty in my life, I was forced to reevaluate the way I'd been living and the work I was doing. The Lord opened doors for me, and I simply obeyed and walked through them. He provided me with the skills to start my "side hustle" in preparation to step out and do something wonderful for others; and myself! In all honesty, though, I was scared. I thought a corporate 9-5 provided me stability and consistency, but while in the middle of an acquisition, I found out that when you work for someone else, you have absolutely no control over what happens to you; and things can change at any time. That realization forced me to trust God more deeply and work harder to turn the stumbling block of acquisition into the stepping-stone of entrepreneurship, and in doing so, helped me reinvent myself to overcome and survive the negative impacts of....the A-word!

WAKE UP AND WIN
Dr. Amicitia (Cita) Maloon–Gibson

ABOUT THE AUTHOR

Dr. Amicitia (Cita) Maloon-Gibson, Ph.D., is the Founder & President of MGAA Professional Development Institute and ATIC & MG Center for Excellence (non-profit). She has dedicated her career to developing others in numerous diverse and inclusive industries. An expert advocate of selecting and developing talent for Executive, Staff and Mid-Level Leadership and business growth success. She has held various Senior Executive leadership roles in industries such as nonprofi and for-profits on board of directors in corporations, ministries, state local and federal governments; Global and throughout Department of Defense.

A retired Executive Leader with three decades of excellence in careers Dr. Amicitia is also a retired Army Lieutenant Colonel, giving 29 year of distinguished service to the nation. She has worked in various leader ship positions throughout the Department of Defense. Her experienc includes serving on local and national boards of directors. Her missior is preparing the next generation of leaders (including future leaders o generations) to be executives and the best leaders possible. She says "Living is a part of giving and leaving a legacy for others."

Contact Dr Cita, she's looking forward to serving you on your journey to becoming a greater results driven leader.

- http://www.johncmaxwellgroup.com/amicitiamaloongibson

- http://www.EmpowermentDoc.com

- http://www.CitaGibson.com

- http://inspireleadgrow.com

CHAPTER 9

WAKE UP AND WIN

Everyone needs motivation in order to be successful. The Word of God is filled with statements meant to motivate us and get us to the place where God wants us in life and service to Him. Today I want you to look with me at Romans 13:11-14 and consider how Paul was inspired by the Holy Spirit to write words to motivate Christians in divine service and Christian action. Be assured of this, we need these words today in the church of our Lord as much as any time in history.

Let's look at Romans 13:11-14: "11 And do this, knowing the time, that now it is high time to awake out of sleep; for now our salvation is nearer than when we first believed. 12 The night is far spent; the day is at hand. Therefore, let us cast off the works of darkness, and let us put on the armor of light. 13 Let us walk properly, as in the day, not in revelry and drunkenness, not in lewdness and lust, not in strife and envy. 14 But put on the Lord Jesus Christ, and make no provision for the flesh, to fulfill its lusts." (NKJV)

In this text, Paul is dealing with the fact that the Christians in Rome were not taking the duty of being faithful Christians seriously. He was calling on them to consider three important things regarding their responsibility to Christ. In writing this Paul is seeking to stir up and wake up the people of God in Rome before it is too late for them to be effective for the Lord. I tell you with seriousness and a broken heart, that we must WAKE UP right now as Christians in America and around the world.

The atheist community is hard at work to corrupt the minds of our youth and Satan has added so many weapons to his arsenal in recent years. Just look at the drug epidemic in America - and around the world, for that matter. In America we are slipping away from God, and our churches are closing their doors in record numbers. Hardly a text can be found in God's Word more appropriate for our generation than the one Paul wrote in Romans 13:11-14.

No matter who we are, we require encouragement and motivation in our lives from time to time. I am reminded of a man who was always late for his dental appointment. One day the nurse called to remind him of his appointment to have a tooth filled that day. He said, "I'll probably be about fifteen minutes late, is that okay?" The nurse said, "Oh, sure, that's okay, but we will not have time to give you your anesthetic." The man arrived fifteen minutes early for the appointment. The thought of not having an anesthetic for his dental procedure cured his lackadaisical attitude and actions.

What will it take to get God's people to be excited and faithful in this modern age? Paul addresses this issue and what he had to say can motivate us today. First, note...

I. SLEEPING

A time to sleep and a time to rest are necessary, but in God's kingdom work we must be alert at all times. A soldier needs sleep, but he can destroy the entire Army if he is sleeping on guard duty. A child needs sleep to do well in school, but no child ever learned anything while sleeping in class. Perhaps the best example regarding the danger of sleeping involves an automobile. Some of the worst traffic accidents in history have occurred because someone fell asleep behind the wheel of a car or truck.

Paul is writing to the Christians in Rome when he tells them that it is high time for them to awake from their sleep. Why is Paul concerned about this issue? Paul says, "...our salvation is nearer than when we first believed." Indeed! Each day we live we are closer to the full and complete redemption to be given to us when our Lord returns. For those Roman Christians, to whom Paul penned this letter, time was very short. Many of them were going to be put to death by Roman authorities – they had very little time to complete their mission before meeting the Lord.

So, what is the danger mentioned by Paul? Is he speaking of actual sleep or is the word he used in our text a symbol of something far more important? Paul was not concerned with the sleep habits of the Christians in Rome. He wasn't against them getting their eight hours of sleep each night.

One thing necessary for people to work, live, worship, and serve God at their best is to have proper rest. Leadership Magazine mentioned a few years ago that up to 45 million people don't get enough sleep in our modern society.

Paul is writing here about something far more important than the number of hours that each Christian sleeps per night. Paul was referring to the lackadaisical problem that was appearing in the lives of believers in Rome – and for that matter the apathetic manner of Christians everywhere in the world during his ministry. He wrote something similar in 1 Thessalonians 5:6, when he penned, "Therefore let us not sleep, as do others; but let us watch and be sober." Why was this such a concern to Paul?

A. A sleeping person cannot see

If we place our minds in neutral gear as we live each day, we fail to see two things: First, we cannot see what God is doing. Second, we cannot see what is happening to our world. We become blind to divine vision and indifferent to satanic activity.

I read a story recently about a man who entered a home in the middle of the night. He went into the room of the parents and took some jewelry while they slept. Then, he went down the hall and kidnapped their twelve-year-old daughter. Thankfully, the girl was able to scream just as the kidnapper was pulling her out the door of the house. The intruder was caught. The only reason the evil man did not get away with his crime was the fact that the parents, and a neighbor, were awakened in time!

Paul had a vision and he saw a world in need of Jesus. He was awake to the danger that faced every living soul. Sadly, I think we are like many of those Roman Christians – we sleep while the world is going out to meet God unprepared. There are few tears for the lost in the church anymore and very few Christians who witness to anyone concerning the coming day of reckoning.

Also, we must ask about what Satan is up to in your church. Oh, you can be sure he is working right there in your fellowship, and among your very best church members. What is God seeking to do in your life and the lives of your fellow believers? You can only know the answers to these questions if you are awake.

In Judges 16:19-20 we read about Samson and Delilah. What did she do in order to ruin the great servant of God? She first put him to sleep! No enemy was strong enough to capture him and cut his hair while he was awake. It was by the use of sleep that she was able, along with her cohorts, to take from the great Samson the strength that God had given him. Listen, dear Christian, Satan is working to dull your senses, to close your eyes, to put you out of commission. No wonder Paul said, "It is high time to awaken out of sleep."

B. A sleeping person cannot think

When you are sleeping, you cannot experience rational thoughts. In fact, you often have crazy dreams that make absolutely no sense. You cannot solve math problems, make out a grocery list or decide on vacation plans while you are snoring like a buzz saw.

In the passage we are considering, Paul reminds the Roman believers that time is shorter than they think. He is seeking to awaken them to something they cannot grasp while being spiritually dull and listless.

One of the great dangers of modern Christianity is that we live in a spiritual world that is "cut and dried." That is, we live in a monotonous, humdrum, and unexciting spiritual form or habit. Like a sleeping person, we go through the hours of spiritual activity, but they are mostly meaningless. They do not move us, stimulate us, or excite us.

Someone was speaking the other day about a day at work. He said, "You know, it was three in the afternoon, and I sat at my desk wondering what I had done all day. For a couple of minutes, I couldn't even remember what I had done since I got to work at eight that morning. After a period of concentration, I began to recall what I had been doing. Whew! I thought I was losing my mind." Then he added, "I guess I had been going through the motions and was sort of sleepwalking through my work." Ah, there is the truth, if you ever heard it! And it is possible for us as believers to do that in our walk and service for God.

We are not really awake. We are going through the motions of activity without the Spirit of God empowering us or working in us. It is high time we awoke from our sleep.

Where was Jonah when the awful nightmare in his life reached the crisis point? He was asleep in the bottom of a ship on the way to Tarshish. It was then the great storm arose, and the mariners came for him. It is interesting that while the worldly sailors were fighting a storm, the backslidden Jonah was sleeping! The world is in trouble and many Christians are sleeping away in the storm. We cannot think properly if we are not alert to all God has to say, all that is going on around us, and all that we are to be doing.

C. A sleeping person cannot pray

When Jesus was in the Garden of Gethsemane, He asked His disciples to watch and pray. After Jesus had prayed for a time, He came back to find them sleeping. As Jesus agonized with sweat drops as blood, His disciples slept.

Sleeping Christians have no idea how to pray because they are oblivious to the spiritual world around them. That night in the garden, the disciples slept because they had no idea the battle Jesus was fighting just a few feet away from them. If we are not awake to God's will, we miss the mark in our prayer lives. I'm not trying to go all spiritual on you in this message, but I am saying that people who say they cannot pray are simply asleep in their souls. Look at the world. Look at the hurting people. Look at what Satan is doing to our society. Look ... oh, wait! I forgot. You can't look because you are asleep!

Wake up, Christian. It's time for us to awaken so we can see, think, and pray like God wants us to at a time like this.

So, we've thought about sleep, now notice secondly...

II. STIRRING

In verse 12 of our text, Paul says that we must "cast off" the works of darkness. This means that we must be stirred – shaken – awakened. I have been a teacher and a student of the gospel for more than 40 years, and I can say without equivocation that there has not been a time in my ministerial life when I believe the people of God have needed a stirring movement from heaven any more than right now!

A. Get Rid of It

The words "cast off" in the text means to remove something – to get rid of something. One might imagine that this means to cast off the night clothes and bed covers. When we awaken from sleep that is what we do. We rid ourselves of the bed coverings and sleep garments so we can get on with the day's activities. Certainly, Paul alluded to this imagery in the text.

We can ascertain that there is still more meant by the words "cast off " that Paul used. We find the one Greek word used for the two words in the text in numerous places in the New Testament. Let's just look at one of them.

In Hebrew 12:1 we read, "...let us lay aside every weight, and the sin which so easily ensnares us..." The writer to the Hebrews was using the idea of a runner who is preparing to run a race. In this passage, he uses the very same word Paul used in our text today. A runner is "stirred" in body and soul to run a race with efficiency and success, so the first thing he does is remove any garment that might encumber his effort. You have never seen a person running a marathon in an overcoat! Likewise, we are being called to stir ourselves so that we might rid our souls of any thought or action that has the potential of slowing us down in our effort to serve the Lord properly and effectively. I was a runner for many years, and I often ran thirty to forty miles per week. Before starting off on a ten-mile run, I had to dress properly, stretch correctly and then pace myself over the long run. Paul is reminding us as Christians that we are runners for Christ. We are to remove encumbering items, stretch out our souls, and make every necessary adjustment so that we might keep moving with God and for God.

What do we need to get rid of in order to serve God better? Think about that for a moment. It is interesting in our day to observe church members and their faithfulness or lack thereof. Any event, activity or interest that comes along easily becomes more important than being faithful to God in worship and Bible study. A child's ballgame or soccer game can take out grandma, granddad, mother, father, brother, sister, and all their friends for a Sunday morning trip to a sports event. Sure, if this was a one-time national championship, that might make sense. But what I'm seeing today is people doing this every week for weeks on end, and it is often for a nine, ten or eleven-year-old child. The child, and other family members, are being taught that God takes a backseat to every other interest in this world. No wonder we can't win this generation to Christ.

We must "stir" ourselves and get rid of things that prohibit us from running the race for Christ as we should. I know that what I'm saying is not popular. It may even hit some people right between the eyes. When the doctor sticks a needle in your arm, it hurts; however, it can save your life. Stir yourselves and rid your lives of those things that keep you from serving God. Wake up before it is too late to do so.

B. Get on With It

Hebrews 12:1-3 reads, "Therefore we also, since we are surrounded by so great a cloud of witnesses, let us lay aside every weight, and the sin which so easily ensnares us, and let us run with endurance the race that is set before us, 2 looking unto Jesus, the author and finisher of our faith, who for the joy that was set before Him endured the cross, despising the shame, and has sat down at the right hand of the throne of God. 3 For consider Him who endured such hostility from sinners against Himself, lest you become weary and discouraged in your souls."

We are not only told to get rid of that which ensnares us but to "run with endurance the race" before us, and to do so by looking unto Jesus who endured the cross. You are to do this lest you become "weary and discouraged in your souls." Ah, there it is again. "Weary!" What are we likely to do when we are weary? Sit down, do nothing, and probably fall sleep!

In the text found in Romans, which we are considering today, we are told to "walk properly." This means that we are to have a walk and life that reflects the Lord who saved us. This has to do with our influence and example to others who may not know the Lord. Paul writes that we are live in the light of day and not like those who do evil deeds in the darkness of night. Dear people, don't you know that the world looks at us and sees that we are in many ways no different than they who do not know or claim to know the Lord. If we do not live awake and stirred in our service for God, we have no witness, no example, and no positive influence on those who are perishing without a Savior.

What we are going to do for the Lord we must do quickly. Time is of the essence. That is exactly what Paul is talking about in this text. Our work for the Lord may end at any moment, with our death or His return. We want to be found faithful to the end, so we must "get on with it!"

So, we've considered sleeping and stirring, but now look at the word ...

III. SHINING

Paul writes that we are to walk "as in the day," which means to be in the light – shining in the light of His glory. We are to reflect the Lord – His glory – His goodness! We are to "put on the armor of light!"

A. Shine forth His Purity

Note that Paul makes clear reference to our living in the light of purity. Paul writes in verse 13, "Let us walk properly, as in the day, not in revelry and drunkenness, not in lewdness and lust..." The life of the world has always been one of "party" and "pleasure." The party is not a reference to simply having a good time, but a reference to a party of drunkenness and wild times. If you think that our generation is worse than those before us, think again. Paul was writing about the tendency in his age of people to give themselves over to the use of narcotics, mostly drink, in order to "feel" good.

A recent report revealed that more Americans are hooked on drugs, including prescription drugs, than any time in our history. We are finding it difficult to cope and drugs and alcohol have become the cure-all for many people. In fact, the drug problem in America is so bad that deaths caused by the overuse of drugs has begun to lower the average age of death. After watching the lifespan of Americans increase year after year, we are now seeing that life-span decline because so many people are dying long before God intended.

There is a problem – alcohol and narcotic drugs don't cure a heart that needs God. Paul knew that what Christians need is to be filled with the Spirit of God and dressed in His armor. Jesus said that believers are to act in ways to show forth the glory of God. We must be dressed in His armor to reflect His light. There simply is no substitute for being filled with God's Spirit – only His Spirit can keep us awake, available and advancing into enemy territory.

B. Shine forth His Peace

Note also that Paul tells us to get rid of envy and jealousy. Sadly, many churches deal with leaders and members who are in conflict with each other. Rather than reflecting the peace of God, they reflect the war that comes from Satan. Listen to me carefully! Satan loves to see a church in conflict. He wants the pastor, staff, leaders, and members to fuss, fume, and fight. He delights in this because it tarnishes the armor and deflects the glory of God. Churches need to have a service for Peace and Love. In that service there ought to be a time when members go to one another and apologize and renew their love for each other. You might think this is a ridiculous idea, but I have called for this publicly in more than one revival in the past, and I've seen what it can do. When people begin to hug, forgive, and pray together, there is a revival of peace. Tears of joy are shared. God is glorified. Jesus is uplifted. The whole body of

Christ is stirred and is reflecting the glory of God when God's peace fills His people!

If we don't get rid of conflict, pride, envy, and jealousy in our churches, we will never see genuine revival take place. We must forgive each other. We must ask for forgiveness where we have been critical of another Christian. We must bury the hatchet – handle and all! Let God's peace shine through us and we will sense an empowering, renewed love and joy. Don't live in denial, acting as if all is well when you know it isn't! Go to those who have hurt you, or to those to whom you've been unkind and open your heart in love. Watch what God will do!

C. Shine forth His Personality

Lastly, Paul says to "...put on the Lord Jesus Christ, and make no provision for the flesh..." Just as Paul told us to cast off our bed clothes, he tells us to put on our heavenly clothes. We are to dress up in the nature and personality of our Savior. We are to shine for His glory to the world.

In essence, Paul tells us to...

Wake Up

Get Up

Clean Up

Dress Up and

Stand Up

Don't you think it is time we did these things? Every true Christian knows that we need to wake up before it is too late.

CONCLUSION

Let me close with a true story from the life of the great missionary, David Livingstone. Some people heard about the great work David Livingstone was doing in Africa, so they wrote to him the following: "Have you found a good road to where you are? If so, we want to know how to send other men to join you." It is said that David Livingstone wrote back, "If you have men who will come only if they know there is a good road, I don't want them. I want men who will come if there is no road at all."

God is looking for some men and women in Christ who will wake up and serve Him walking through a valley, climbing a mountain, wading through deep waters, stepping through fire – or even carrying a cross up a lonely hill. How many today are willing to step out and renew an alert, awakened heart to Christ? Or perhaps, to wake from your sleep and give your heart to Jesus who walked up the hill called Calvary to die in your place.

Tea Time – Happiness, Healing and Harmony

Tina Hunter

ABOUT THE AUTHOR

Tina Hunter is a Published Author, Empowerment Speaker, and CEO of Smoochez Boutique all while maintaining an executive position within the Federal Government. Tina is also a radio co-host and the visionary behind the Motivate and Empower (M.E.) movement where she serves and supports emerging entrepreneurs. Tina also hosts annual networking events and creates platforms for thought leaders to infuse their brands and provide tools to educate, inspire and encourage people. Tina is committed to acknowledging and bringing out the best in everyone she encounters.

In Tina's weekly live virtual sessions titled "Tea Time with Tina," catering to her "Fearlessly Me!" tribe, she uses her daily experiences to motivate and empower. As the owner of Smoochez Boutique, Tina takes delight in the opportunity to highlight beauty internally and externally. Her motto is " it's time to rise up and face your fears even when it seems impossible." Tina's expertise as a stylist led her to initiate the brand "High Heel Hustler" representing a movement for entrepreneurial women who boldly live out their journey with courage and confidence. The High Heel Hustler initiative salutes and promotes focused oriented women who deliver results and solutions all while maintaining style and grace.

Tina has spoken on various platforms, summits, and panels. Her sole mission is to inspire women to shift their mindsets, declare their greatness, walk in faith, and make the conscious decision to confidently fear less and faith more. Tina's vulnerability of sharing her story motivates and empowers women to rise up and face the fears even when things seem impossible. Her vibrant personality and inviting tone ignites a spark among her audiences to take inspired action and release the false self-limiting beliefs. Tina's personal story is one of determination and resilience that empowers others to live out the best version of themselves. Tina also hosts vision board events, coaching sessions, and webinars. Her focused topics include empowering women to be fearless and moving them to their next level.

CHAPTER 10

TEA TIME – HAPPINESS, HEALING AND HARMONY

I know you're wondering what Tea Time is and why I decided to write about it.

Well, it was years ago, when I first became a mom. Being a young single mother of two at the time wasn't such an easy task. Especially, while trying to build a career and do school at the same time. I found myself doing my daily tasks during the day and a lot of times after getting the kids off to bed, I would be so tired all I could do was shower, pray and hit the sheets for the night. As time went on and I started feeling myself as a mature mother raising her kids and chilling in my own beautifully designed 3-bedroom apartment. It was time I started creating a zen space just for me and my favorite girlfriends. So, I did just that and we would gather with food, we would cook, and of course have drinks of everyone's choice. Mine was always tea of some sort. Not saying I ended the night with it.

Fast forward as years went by, tea was still my number one go-to first thing in the morning and last thing at night. I know you're still wondering what's so doggone special about this Tea Time thing. Before being introduced to real exotic tasty teas, I was addicted to regular caffeinated Lipton tea, which was on point for me at any given time that I needed to be still and relax my mind. Tea Time saved my life in 2017 after my beautiful mother gained her wings to heaven. God led me to start an online platform for a group of women called *Tea Time with Tina*. I was afraid because that meant that I had to be online in front of people and I didn't know what they would think about the concept or if anyone would be interested. So, I got started and women were so open and ready for Tea Time. I had so many women say they loved my weekly platform and would be ready every Tuesday. I would show up with my cup of tea and have Tea Time with a community of women, making sure they had their tea. We talked about everything under the sun.

As I was going through my grief and healing journey, I realized that this was bigger than me. With the information and me just showing up consistently, the women were transforming as well. I started getting back so much positive feedback that I decided to take Tea Time and share it on other social media platforms like Facebook, Instagram, and YouTube. This was the best thing I could have ever done.

Tea Time was a connection to other phenomenal women that needed to share their stories and feel like they were being heard as well.

Tea Time was a connection for women to learn new skills and make money while learning.

Tea Time was a connection for women to feel safe and not worry about being judged on how they looked or spoke while speaking their truth via-social media or in person.

Tea Time was a connection for great opportunities in the work force and entrepreneurship world. Sisters were not afraid to share their knowledge and help the sisters grow.

Tea Time was also, a connection for women to support women making money as they shared their gifts and talents as sisters would support by purchasing their products and services. Also, would share their information with new clientele as well.

So, as you can see my Tea Time was spent a little differently most times. Don't get me wrong because I am a real Tea Time girl, I still sit quietly and have a few cups of tea a day. In a nutshell what I am saying is Tea Time is a way for me to do Gods work along with something that I truly enjoy doing and that is motivation and empowering other sisters in the community. So, as you go through your day, please make sure you take time out for self and have you a nice hot cup of tea and allow it to work on you from the inside out. It will relax you, give you time to sit and get your thoughts together and it will have you smack your lips saying how good it taste. Especially, when you start experimenting with new flavors like peach and orange mixed with a cinnamon stick to top it off.

As I close out what Tea Time is really about, it is a place to invite someone in and show them a great time without telling them you're going to show them a great time. It's a safe space to smile and let the real you out. And it can be free if you're at home enjoying the moment or if you happen to be out doing Tea Time it's a very inexpensive habit to have in a loving way. So, as I close this message up. I say to you "Go have Tea Time with that special person..." they probably need it.

From me to you - go create your Tea Time and don't forget a sprinkle of cinnamon and a slice of lemon.

DON'T FORGET TO REMEMBER!
Valerie Marie Howard-Jones

ABOUT THE AUTHOR

Valerie Marie Howard-Jones is a DC native and is the CEO of Apostle Val Ministries and the Founder and Senior Pastor of Restoring Life Family Community Center of Bowie, MD.

Apostle Val, was licensed to preach the Gospel in 1994 by Bishop Kevin V. Gresham, Sr. of the Greater St. John Church of Upper Marlboro, MD and ordained in 2006 by Bishop Mark Anthony Wilson of the

Greater Destiny Kingdom Ministries of Baltimore, MD. She was consecrated as Pastor in 2007 by Bishop Wilson and again in 2011 by Bishop Ernest C. Dawson of Rehoboth New Life Church Alliance of Clinton, MD. She was concentrated as Apostle in 2022 by Apostle Kim Meekins of Spirit of Christ Global Ministries of Richmond, VA

Apostle Val is the Co-CEO of the *SIBTT Literary Group* (Sister I've Been There Too), which is a ministry birthed out of the book "Sister, I've Been There Too! *But I Came Back to Get You!*" SIBTT is a compilation of testimonies, written by nine very different women and one man, about just how good God really is! In addition, Apostle Val is also a co-author in the recently released "*Empowered to Win 2nd and 3rd Editions,*" which are another compilation of testimonies and encouragement for the Body of Christ! These writings have made Apostle Val an Amazon #1 Best Seller nationally and internationally. Additionally, Apostle Val was a contributing author on *A Drink from His Well* (2008), her first published writing.

Apostle Valerie is the Director of Pastoral Counseling, and Prayer for *I AM My Sister's Keeper* as well as Vice President of the Board of Directors (NC), Vice President of the Board of Directors for the *Walbrook Warriors Alumni Association* (MD), as well as serving on several non-profit organizations in a variety of leadership capacities.

Apostle Val can be heard every Saturday at 3:00 PM for *A Drink from His Well* broadcast on 1350 AM WLLY () in Wilson, NC., Friday

Nights, via Zoom Meetings for *Let's Talk, Real Talk,* and Monday through Friday on Facebook Live for *Daily Meditations.*

Apostle Val holds an associate degree in Office Management, a Bachelor of Science degree in Criminal Justice, with a minor in Corrections, and a Master of Science degree in Public Administration, with a minor in Legal Studies. Apostle Val is employed by the federal government as a Management Analyst.

Favorite scripture: Revelation 12:11 "And they overcame by the blood of the Lamb and the word of their testimony, and they did not love their lives unto death."

Apostle Val is the mother of two daughters – AlNetta and Jessica: three bonus daughters – Lora, Julisa, and Jasmine. Three bonus sons: Deron, Raymond, and Anthony, two sons-in-law: Tino and BJ.

CHAPTER 11

DON'T FORGET TO REMEMBER!

Hebrews 12:1 "Wherefore seeing we also are compassed about with so great a cloud of witnesses, let us lay aside every weight, and the sin which doth so easily beset us, and let us run with patience the race that is set before us." (KJV)

About twenty years ago, as I was preparing to preach my second sermon, I was completing some research; God always has me searching beyond the norm or the comfortable. You see, like you and most of us who are anointed, appointed, ordained, and gifted in the uncomfortable gifts; you know the ones that make people nervous because they can't control them or us. There have been some challenges in discovering ME. I've never fit comfortably into anyone's box, especially if I knew you were trying to box me in for whatever the reason. All too often, the religious stigmas that we place on others is so subtle and routine, that we don't even notice it or see it coming. We've become so indoctrinated in the things of man's church, that when God deals with us outside of the box man is comfortable with, we tend to forget that we are *"studying to shew ourselves approved unto God, so that we can be workmen, rightly dividing the word of truth"* (2 Tim. 2:15 KJV).

Man's truth, traditions, expectations, and boarders, usually have nothing to do with God and everything to do with how they see us, use us, and tolerate us. Tolerance. Yes, tolerance is something that we talk about, but very seldom walk in effectively. See, as humans and religious individuals, we are not comfortable, for the most part, with things, people, and places that we cannot control. For a child of the Most High, that's an interesting place to be in. How do I surrender my heart, mind, and my will and be in control at the same time?

I came across this article about how baby giraffes are born. Apparently, mother giraffes don't lay down to give birth, as with most mammals, but remain standing up. If that wasn't strange enough, mothers are pregnant for 14 to 15 months with just one baby and at birth, baby giraffes fall from their mother's womb to the ground. This fall can be about a 6-foot drop (Snyder, 2018). If the drop doesn't shake them into alertness, the mother begins to kick the calf until he/she gets up on their own feet.

Apparently one of the major reasons that nature has giraffes fall into life in such a manner is, due to their surroundings, other predators, and unseen dangers, they need to be able to get up, move, eat, and run, if necessary, very quickly. When your first introduction into life is one of pain, you won't soon forget how to get back up again. You won't soon forget the reality of your surroundings, and you won't soon forget what the enemy looks like once you have experienced him on any level. As a child of God, walking, moving, living and working in the Kingdom, we cannot forget to remember who God is, what He's done in our lives, how He saved us, where we were in the body, mind, and heart when He came to see about us and saved our soul! Yeah, don't forget to remember your process, predestined destination, and powerful testimony!

On this road to salvation, worship, the knowledge of God, and our "expected end" in God, we fight and fight for freedom; the ability to breath outside of the realm of pain, pressure, and punishment only to get to the shore, take a deep breath and then end up allowing ourselves to get sucked back into webs of deceit, dishonesty, depression, and desperation all for the sake of love and acceptance by individuals who refuse to heal, be set-free, or truly be delivered. We tell ourselves that we are being a "good Christian" and that THIS IS what Jesus would do, because that's what we've been told for as long as we can remember. The constant battles, feelings of lack, the awareness that I will never be good enough in the eyes of some, the lies, rejection, quiet – dark conversations that yield nothing but pain and depression. Many of us have endured that and some, all under the umbrella of "Christianity," religion-ship, control, and manipulation. Only to come out on the other side of through, and someone decides that we still are not good enough. Something, although usually when we get to this place in our walk with God, we have no idea what, but something must change.

The winter of '83, after I had graduated high school and had begun perusing my degree, I went on a ski trip with a dear friend of mine and their family. Once on the mountain I went shopping and found a plaque, that I purchased, and it has been with me for over 40 years. The plaque was a quote from Mother Teresa, and she wrote, "We the willing led by the unknowing, are doing the impossible for the ungrateful. We have done so much, with so little, for so long, we are now qualified to do anything, with nothing." (Teresa, n.d.) That quote: that thing right there, began a change in me that is still unfolding.

I honestly thought the quote was funny and since I worked for the federal government and was a little frustrated with them at the time; it was cool to post in my office. Little did I know that quote would walk with me for forty years or better and is still impacting my life today. Why, might you ask? Because it helps me to remember that we are all human and will do and say what humans do and speak. If I'm wounded and I never seek healing, I speak from my wounds. If I'm depressed, and never talk to anyone, I speak from my depression. If I have childhood trauma, and many of us do, that I've hidden because I was told "what goes on in the house stays in the house," and I've never allowed myself to verbalize my trauma, I speak and act out of that unhealed place. We can only give what we have and if all I have is hurt, pain, rejection, and darkness that has not been addressed, released, or even spoken, no matter how much I do, if I refuse to heal for real, I can only give the unhealed, churchy version of me to anyone who asks me.

Beloved, I know it doesn't seem like it right now, with all that is going on in the world and around you, but your best days are still in front of you! I don't care what they (whoever "they" are) think they've done, or what they are planning on doing, what God has for you is for you! AND, you and I have just have to understand that everything and everyone we love can't go where God is taking us. No shade. No bullying. No manipulation. No, we won't do to them what all they have done and tried to do to us! We, you, and I, can be exactly who God says we are without intentionally hurting anyone or allowing them to hurt, distract, or stop us! We can, and will, walk in the power of His might! We will show forth the praises of Him that has called and sent us! Glory to God!!

There are a few things that we need to remember as we continue to ask, knock, and seek God for who we are, what we are ordained and gifted to do, and do it in love. One – Don't forget to remember that God is not like man, and He won't devalue, disrespect, depress, or destroy you! – *Deuteronomy 31:6 (KJV) Be strong and of a good courage, fear not, nor be afraid of them: for the LORD thy God, He it is that doth go with thee; He will not fail thee, nor forsake thee.* God is not man, He will never leave you, turn His back on you, lie to you, or trade you in for a better model. There is a level in God that most men won't ever touch simply because we forget to remember that *God is not a man, that He should lie; neither the son of man, that He should repent: hath He said, and shall He not do it? Or hath He spoken, and shall He not make it good? (Numbers 23:19 KJV).* In the words of my unt Dessie, we've got to stop trying to assign human attributes to a Divine God! Many of us can't imagine having the level of intimacy and communication with God that He has intended and provided simply because of our relationships, or lack thereof with the human beings in our lives. People we have trusted with all of us, and they have tried to destroy all of us, simply because they cannot control, manipulate, or pimp our gifts and anointing. But God!

n our attempt to feel better about who we are, how we've lived, choices and decisions we've made, and what we refuse to release from our hearts to God, we try to assign a level of humanity to God, which is beneath Him. God's ways are higher than our ways; His thoughts are higher than our thoughts, and instead of us trying to bring Him down to our level of comfort, we've got to learn how come up to where He is uncomfortable and all. The thing is this, why bring God down to our level? If it was so good at our level, we wouldn't need God. I'm just saying, don't forget to remember where God has brought you from. Don't forget to remember those sleepless nights it took to get you here, why turn back now? Don't forget to remember that you are fearfully and wonderfully made in God's image. Don't forget to remember that man might not be able to see you the way God created you, because they can't even handle what they see about themselves.

Two – Don't forget to remember that God has a plan for your life, that just might not add up to the plans man (mommy, daddy, spouse, etc.) has for your life. *Jeremiah 29:11 (KJV) For I know the thoughts that I think toward you, saith the LORD, thoughts of peace, and not of evil,* *give you an expected end.* Human expectations are one of the bigge: disappointments a heart can endure. We want people to love us. W want people to like us; understand us and give us back some level c the love and respect we believe we have given to them. In the absenc of that love and respect, rather than walk away and throw our hanc up, we usually dig in and go for broke trying to convenience them tha we are worthy of their love and attention. An unsurrendered heart ca: never love you the way you desire, need, and expect to be loved. Peopl can't give you what they don't have. YOU keep moving forward. YOL keep trusting God, even and especially in the uncomfortable places YOU keep loving and praying for them, without stopping, waiting dragging, and pulling. Don't forget to remember that you don't hav heaven nor hell to put anyone in and as a child of God, that shouldn' even be a consideration. Don't forget to remember that it takes si: months to mind my business and six months to leave yours alon because it takes twelve months and 365 days a year to perfect ME Trust God with you and them and keep moving forward.

Three – Don't forget to remember that everything you've ever felt done, or had done to you, God is using to build YOU! Mold YOU: Shape YOU! Bring YOU to and expected end in HIM! *Romans 8:28 (KJV) And we know that all things work together for good to them that love God, to them who are the called according to His purpose.* Not one ingredient used to create you will be wasted! No one wants to hear that the blood, sweat, and tears they've gone through to be who they are to-

ay, is working for your good, but you ought to! At some point in your
ourney, it should be good news that all the pain, darkness, and drama
f life has an expected end and great purpose. That every tear you've
ver shed, had an assignment in your life and it wasn't destruction but
levation, exposure, and blessings. Don't you ever forget to remember
hat God created you on purpose! Don't forget to remember that you
ill never be everyone's cup of tea and it's their loss. Don't you forget
o remember the tears, lack, oppression, suppression, and depression
hat God has delivered you from. Not so you can rehearse the hurt, but
o you celebrate the victories! Don't forget to remember the sleepless
ights, and how *He that keepeth Israel shall neither slumber nor sleep.
The LORD is thy keeper: The LORD is thy shade upon thy right hand
Psalm 121:4-5 KJV).* Don't forget to remember that God will honor
our sacrifice and your surrender! *Mark 10:29-31 (KJV) [29] And Jesus
answered and said, Verily I say unto you, There is no man that hath
eft house, or mother, or wife, or children, or lands, for my sake, and the
ospels' [30] But he shall receive an hundredfold now in this time, houses,
nd brethren, and sisters, and mothers, and children, and lands, with
ersecutions; and in the world to come eternal life. [31] But many that are
irst shall be last; and the last first.*

ourth, and finally – Don't forget to remember that the success of
our relationship with God and your Godly destiny in God is a daily
rocess that YOU control, build on, and invest in. *Romans 12:1-3
KJV) [1] I beseech you therefore, brethren, by the mercies of God, that ye
resent your bodies a living sacrifice, holy, acceptable unto God, which is*

your reasonable service. ²And be not conformed to this world: but be ₁ transformed by the renewing of your mind, that ye may prove what , that good, and acceptable, and perfect will of God. ³For I say, throug₁ the grace given unto me, to every man that is among you, not to thin₁ of himself more highly than he ought to think; but to think soberl₁ according as God hath dealt to every man the measure of faith.

Every single day of your life, you are worthy of God's next for you! Ye₁ you made some mistakes. Yes, you spoke out of turn. Yes, some of th₁ choices, places, people, and situations you've gotten yourself into wa₁ simply mind blowing. But God! Don't forget to remember to tak₁ every experience; the good, the bad, and the ugly and put the Word o₁ God to work in your life, your heart, and your mind so you can rene₁ your mind in God, the things of God, and the Word of God daily! Yo₁ can't lose with what we use, but we must use it! We are all given ₁ measure of faith, and even if that faith is the size of a mustard seed, it' starting somewhere. Don't forget to remember to give yourself som₁ grace!

Much like the baby giraffe, we won't soon forget our entrance int₁ the things of God. Very few of us in today's world, have warm an₁ fuzzy stories about how we came into salvation, our conversion int₁ the things of God, or even the battles we fought to get to where we ar₁ today. Reality hits different when it's you! Loneliness hits differentl₁ when it's your friends that walked away and your family that turne₁ their backs on you because they prefer the wounded version rather tha₁ he healed version of you. Rejection hits different when the uncondi-onal love you give or expect is not forthcoming, because those who sist on it from you refuse to learn how to give it themselves. Yeah, ain hits differently when your expectations for other behaviors are set o high. We must take our emotions out of God's business and take fe, as He has ordained it for us, as the children of God, on God's terms.

Don't forget to remember, that you were fearfully and wonderfully ade in God's image! Don't forget to remember, that God has an xpected end for you that might not look like what man is comfortable ith from you. Don't forget to remember that most humans have no dea what real love is, and when you find it in God, don't be surprised they don't recognize it, appreciate it, or return it. Don't forget to emember that your relationship with God wasn't a conference call and ou don't need everyone's buy-in to be in with Him. Don't forget o remember, that no matter how much the world hates you, God's ove for you will never die, is unmatched by man, and is complete; God's love will heal, set you free, and deliver you all at the same time! Don't forget to remember that God so loved you, that He gave His only egotten son, so that you could have life, and life more abundantly! Don't forget to remember how to live! PEACE!

REFERENCES:

King James Holy Bible (n.d.) retrieved from https://www.bibleg e HYPERLINK "https://www.biblegateway.com/"w HYPERLIN "https://www.biblegateway.com/"ay.com

Snyder, C. L. (Nov. 2018). 10 Of the Strangest Ways Animals Gi Birth. *Insider*. Retrieved from Mother Teresa of Calcutta (n.d.) quot fancy. Retrieved from

https://quotefancy.com/quote/868978/Mother-Teresa-We-the-willi g-led-by-the-unknowing-are-doing-the-impossible-for-the

Same Person, New Purpose
Kristian Gregory-Lee

About the Author

Kristian Gregory-Lee is an international best-selling author and speaker. She wrote and published her first book at the age of 9 years old. Her book is entitled, *Broken Peace*. She is the contributing author of the Book Series, *Empowered to Win, 1ˢᵗ Edition*, *Empowered to Win, 2ⁿᵈ Edition* and *Empowered to Win, 4ᵗʰ Edition*. She graduated from Frederick Douglass High with a 4.0 GPA. She graduated from Salisbury University with her bachelor's degree in business administration with high honors and was the Homecoming Queen of 2012. She currently teaches choreography (Cheerleading) at James Madison Middle School. She has spoken on several platforms and was awarded a chance to go to Tokyo for a business trip. She has assisted and conducted several conferences as a Zoom Director.

She is the Manager and Zoom Director of AGD Publishing Services, LLC. She is a Legacy Speaker at the first Women Empowered to Win Summit. She loves traveling, reading and good conversations.

CHAPTER 12

SAME PERSON, NEW PURPOSE

"But the plans of the Lord stand firm forever, the purposes of his heart through all generations." Psalms 33:11 KJV

As a young adult in my younger years, I always believed that once I found my purpose it would forever stay that same. I thought that once I found my purpose things would fall in place. But now I realize that I'm the same person with a new purpose

What does purpose mean to me, well first dictionary.com states that purpose means:

1. the reason for which something exists or is done, made, used, etc.

2. an intended or desired result; aim; goal.

Well, I started looking back over my life and I wrote several goals that I wanted to achieve. We all have goals that we want to achieve but you must:

1. Write the vision down.

2. Gain clarity on it meaning research.

3. Decide how you want to proceed.

4. And then act on it.

But if you don't act on it, you may just be holding onto a dream or a goal that you will never achieve.

So, when I said that my title was SAME PERSON, NEW PURPOSE

It was because I had changed my goals over time.

I was slowly evolving into the women I believe that God was calling me to be.

SAME PERSON, NEW PURPOSE

- I love reading, so I wrote a book published by AGD Publishing Services

- I love to cook, so I started my TikTok channel teaching others how to cook.

- I love sports so I joined a volleyball team.

- I wanted to finish college, so I earned my bachelor's degree.

- I achieved my goal in the office of becoming an executive retail manager and leading a team for several years.

- I love giving back to the community, so I joined a great bikers club, and we constantly give back to the community and yes, we also have some fun times together, too.

- I wanted to own my own home and I achieved that Goal of being a first-time homeowner.

SAME PERSON, NEW PURPOSE

Every goal that I pursued, achieved, and accomplished.

- I wrote the vision down.

- I read my daily scriptures.

- I stayed focused on my goals.

Although I was young, I was guided by my parents on how to achieve my goals by staying focused, staying the course, and believing in myself.

Now as an adult, having achieved many of my goals that others thought were out of my reach, I have learned to set my standard so high that it seems impossible for most but achievable in my eyes.

SAME PERSON, NEW PURPOSE

I'm constantly setting new goals for myself as I evolve into a higher/stronger version of myself. I believe that you must go hard for what you desire or become stagnant and leave with regret.

If you don't decide on your path/purpose in life, life will decide for you.

SAME PERSON, NEW PURPOSE

When I say "same person new purpose," I mean I changed the narrator and the words that I spoke over my life. When you a child you think as a child when you become an adult you must adjust and refocus your purpose to make the rules for your journey.

As I close, I want to leave with you that my motto for this year as I pursue my new purpose, is that you should make it your new goal, your new journey starts by being intentional about making a difference, making an impact in your own life.

MAKING AN IMPACT BY FULFILLING YOUR LIFE'S PURPOSE!

Dr. Essie McKoy

ABOUT THE AUTHOR

Dr. McKoy received her Doctorate in Education (Ed.D.) and an Educational Specialist Degree (Ed. S.) in Educational Leadership from the University of North Carolina at Greensboro, a master's degree in Middle Grades Education from Appalachian State University, and a Bachelor of Science Degree in Special Education with certification in Learning Disabilities from Winston-Salem State University. She has additional areas of certification in Public School Administration/Principalship, Curriculum and Instruction with a concentration in English, and the Superintendency. Her dissertation topic, "A Study of Elementary Principals' Perceptions of Accountability and Leadership in an Era of High Stakes Testing," is a foundational part of her book, "The Heart of School Transformation: My Journey into Transforming Urban Schools." She attended The Urban Superintendent's Program at Howard University and The American Association of School Administrators and received the National Superintendent's Certification.

In addition, she attended Harvard University's Public Education Leadership Project Program and many other leadership programs throughout the nation, including the Wake Forest University Leadership Program for Public Engagement, The Distinguished Leadership Program and the Distinguished Leadership Digital Learning Program at North Carolina State University, The Principals' Executive Program – Leadership Program for Assistant Principals at the University of North Carolina at Chapel Hill and received the Program's Outstanding Academic Achievement Award and she graduated from the Principals' Executive Program – Leadership Program for New Principals at the University of North Carolina at Chapel Hill where she received the prestigious Jack McCall Award. Dr. McKoy also attended the Mastering Leadership Dynamics Program with the BB&T Institute, as well as three other programs at BB&T. In addition, she was accepted into The National Scholars Honor Society. A highlight of her career is that she was selected by Winston Salem State University as the Education Alumni Achiever Recipient.

Dr. McKoy began her teaching career at an alternative middle school and later taught a "regular" middle school. She served as assistant principal at the elementary level before becoming the principal of two elementary schools. She worked as an instructor at the Math and Science Academy of Excellence at Winston-Salem State University and worked as an Adjunct Professor at NC A&T State University and ITT Technical Institute and served as a Hybrid Instructor at George Mason University. Furthermore, she served as an Executive Director/Principal at the middle school level and has experience at the high school level in the area of special education as a Department Chair. Her experience spans from pre-K through college and she uses her experience and knowledge to continue to make an impact in the field of education! Dr. McKoy was nominated for the AASA Women in School Leadership Award with the Bill and Melinda Gates Foundation. In addition, she received the Educator of the Year Award and The Executive Citation of Anne Arundel County Maryland Award. Dr. McKoy has been featured in COPA Style, K.I.S.H., BSM, SwagHer, Glambitious, PowerHouse Global, She Speaks, Creating Your Seat at the Table, and UP WORDS (Edutopia) magazines. She has received many accolades and recognitions for her accomplishments throughout her extensive career. In 2021, she was named COPA Style Magazine Woman of the Year!

Dr. McKoy is known as an educational guru who served as a transformational leader and improved the academic performance and success indicators of all the schools she has led. She is proud of the fact that both elementary schools became Piedmont Triad Signature Schools-the highest growth schools! Her mission is to continue to ignite the passion in others and make a profound impact in the field of education and in the lives of others!

She is the President and CEO of her own Educational Consulting Company, Dr. Essie Speaks, LLC. She has travelled the nation to do speaking engagements and is an Amazon nine-times Best-selling author. Dr. McKoy has written extensively and continues to contribute to a wide variety of nationwide writing projects. She has written as an author, contributing author, and a foreword author. Some of her books are: The Heart of School Transformation; My Journey into Transforming Urban Schools, Coaching Champions- How to understand the players before giving the plays; A Guide to Improvement and Success, Women of Virtue: Walking in Excellence, Leadership Tidbits, and The Grylfriend Code Sorority Edition, Vision and Purpose; Inspiring Our Community, and Women Who Lead; Extraordinary Women with Extraordinary Achievements – Featuring School Principals.

In addition, she continues to work in her area of expertise for a local school district in the DMV and is the Lead Education Writer for Vision and Purpose Lifestyle Magazine! Furthermore, you will hear Dr. McKoy every Sunday at 5:30 PM EST, hosting her #1 Podcast Show, Dr. Essie Speaks! She is a member of Alpha Kappa Alpha Sorority Incorporated!She invites you to visit her web site at www.dressiespeaks.com and keep abreast of updates on all social media platforms.

CHAPTER 13

MAKING AN IMPACT BY FULFILLING YOUR LIFE'S PURPOSE!

Having the mindset that you are already "Empowered to Win," is just the beginning of the process of fulfilling your life's purpose! Our Higher Power has given us a great purpose and we need to use it to impact others and to make a positive difference in the lives of others. Our purpose in life is truly the reason for our existence. We must live out our mission and fulfill the vision predestined for us. "For I know the plans I have for you," declares the LORD, "plans to prosper you and not to harm you, plans to give you hope and a future." (Jeremiah 29:11, NIV)

Furthermore, I believe the mission of our lives is to carry out the important assignment(s) designed especially for us. The vision of our life allows us to imagine and see the things we want to bring to existence and create in your own reality. Our purpose derives from our vision and our mission and gives us the drive to pursue what we believe we need to do with our lives. All three, vision, mission, and purpose are interwoven to help guide every aspect of our life. It gives us the insight to make decisions, influences our behavior, helps us to create oals, navigates us towards a sense of direction and provides the overall meaning for our lives. When we have purpose, we can see it displayed in every aspect of our life and it gives us the sense of life is worthy to be lived to its fullest, a sense of who we are, a sense of where we belong in his universe, and a sense of being completely fulfilled.

have spent thirty-five plus years of my life serving in the field of education touching every level from pre-K to college and still answering the call, fulfilling my purpose! Who knew it would impact every facet of my personal life and propel me to seek more degrees? Who knew it would lead me to places I have never been and positions I could not have imagined? Who knew it would give me an opportunity to attend prestigious colleges and universities across the nation? Who knew it would allow me to receive many accolades, recognition, and awards in becoming an award-winning educator? Who knew the love of education would have such a great impact on my own children? Who knew I would start at one place and end up at another place? Who knew the call to remain steady and impact students who needed the most would create depth in me? Who knew that so many wonderful opportunities would present itself where I get to make a greater impact on this journey? Who knew it would be an element that would not only impact the lives of students, families, and communities, but impact even my own grandchild? Who knew that it would give me the platform to be a voice in the field of education? Who knew it would allow me the opportunity to become a ten times Amazon best-selling author and a two times international bestselling author? Who knew it would allow me to share my perspectives, insights, and ideas in prominent magazine, Vision, and Purpose Lifestyle Magazine? Who knew it would lead me to sharing via my weekly podcast, Dr. Essi Speaks, where I get to share not only about educational topics, but help to inspire, motivate, and uplift others? Who knew I would start my own educational consulting company? Who knew my journey would allow me to share about God being my anchor, my rock, and my source of inspiration? Who knew that I would have this type of impact?

Of course, I could not see then all that was planned for me, but I stayed the course and worked hard all along the way. I wanted to be the best, do my best, and give my best. I believe that if you extend yourself and do things that you believe are impossible, you will create the best version of yourself! I believe it was already predestined and all connected. I could not see all the puzzle pieces standing separately, but gradually they joined together to create this version of my purpose. As long as I live and as long as I keep growing and giving, I will continue to evolve, and my purpose will continue to evolve. I just had to travel the journey to get to the next destination, open the next door, and step into the next opportunity! What is so amazing is that I just started with the seed of becoming a teacher and throughout the journey, I saw a need to me to be more involved, to grow myself, to lend my skills in areas that some educator did not want to tap into, and to continue to answer the call along the unchartered paths. I know my purpose is tied directly to the fact that education, no matter what form, is my calling. Teaching and earning are my gifts. Motivating and inspiring others is my passion. Serving others in a multitude of ways is my purpose!

If you are starting out trying to find your purpose in life start with that initial thought that was planted in your heart and spirit! Start with what motivates and inspires you! Start with what gives you a sense of satisfaction, the thing that comes naturally, the thing that you are interested in the most, and the thing that brings you inner peace! Start with the thing that keeps you asking what more can I learn about this, what more can I do to make an impact in this area, the thing that uplifts you, the thing that keeps you on the path to self-discovery, the thing that may keep you awake at night because you have the next discovery, that next challenge to tackle, and the thing that never allows you to become bored or complacent.

You are on the right track! Do not give up and do not give in! Always keep going, keep believing, keep seeking that next opportunity, keep the internal flames burning, be true to yourself, do not compare yourself to anyone else, keep educating yourself, and keep developing your skills and abilities. Trust me, you will be amazed at what presents itself to you, what opportunities you decide to take advantage of, what doors will open when you think they are shut, what people and provisions will be waiting for you, where it will lead, and the impact you will make in fulfilling your life's purpose!

OVERCOMING CHALLENGES AND BUILDING RESILIENCE

Shirley Murphy

ABOUT THE AUTHOR

Shirley Murphy is a Nigerian Journalist based in Abuja, Nigeria's federal capital city. She is currently the Publisher of Global Labor Events and Business Magazine (GLEBM), an online independent specialized publication; she is a TV show Host and a media Consultant, as well as an international speaker. She has authored three books, "The Ideal Parents," "5 Steps to Purpose Actualization" and "The Power of

Praise". She is the brain behind two Non-Governmental Organiza
tions (NGOs), Proud Parents International and Women Reach Out
with God Initiative (WROWGI). She believes in collaborating and
supporting the advancement of women across the world. Shirley is a
Life and Family Therapist, who has transformed the lives of many
especially women and girls in Nigeria. She is very passionate about
women's education and Empowered to ensure that women all over the
world become more visible and in control of their lives. She is extremely
compassionate and passionate in giving hope to many women in her
sphere of influence. She is blessed to have both a loving husband and
devoted children.

CHAPTER 14

OVERCOMING CHALLENGES AND BUILDING RESILIENCE

We often face challenges that test our strength, Faith, determination, and resilience. These obstacles can appear in different forms. However, it is through these challenges that we have the opportunity to grow, evolve, and ultimately break barriers that hold us back. In this chapter, I'll explore the power of overcoming challenges and building resilience, offering inspiration and guidance to those on their journey of personal transformation.

In whatsoever you may be going through in life, you must know that God is able to pull you out victoriously. When you have this belief, nothing can keep you down. For us as Christians, God promised to be with us always. He said when we pass through the fire and waters, He will be with us because He knew that situations that seem like fire, so hot and threatening, will come our way, but hold on, look up to Him, and He will see you through.

We often hear that obstacles and challenges do not always come to break us but to make us better in every area that was tested. Though it may sound easier with words, it is sometimes difficult to agree with this statement, but sincerely, it is the truth, and it all has to do with our mindsets and who our Trust is on. Do you trust and depend on your ability to overcome every challenge, or do you fix your eye on the one that can pull you out with evidence of a breakthrough? you are to embrace challenges as an opportunity to learn because when you fail in that project or face disappointment, God is saying, slow down and learn the lessons that are in it. Because of where he is taking you. God is expecting you to stoop down and see him in the making.

The simple word Failure is a challenge that you need to overcome; how do you do that? by changing your mindset. Failing in life helps us to build resilience. The more we forget, the more resilient we become. To achieve great success, we must know resilience. Because if we think that we're going to succeed on the first try, or even the first few tries, then we're sure to set ourselves up for a far more painful failure.

I have failed more times than I'd like to admit. And I'm not talking about small failures; I'm talking about the losses that rock your world, completely altering the landscape of your relationships, finances, and mental well-being.

And I can't say that I particularly enjoy failing, but failure, through its life-altering lessons, makes us into better people.

Failure is life's great teacher; nature's chisel that chips away at all the excess, stripping down egos as it molds and shapes us through divine intentions.

It's through failure that we learn the most significant lessons that life can teach us. I now have the lineup of those experiences to mentor others and today become more resilient because it did not stop me from moving forward but empowered me to become more.

Building resilience starts from within, and emotional stability forms the foundation of our ability to overcome challenges. And it has a lot to do with how we process challenges when they come our way. Do you allow it to drain you, or do you give them a safe space and also be able to keep your peace? These are questions that only you can answer; as you are reading this chapter, know that challenges can bring about stress to our emotional well-being. Therefore, carefully sieving everything is vital to your overall health.

Every journey towards breaking barriers and building resilience is complete with the support of others. You should be able to build or connect yourself to a strong support system. It explores the power of collaboration, mentorship, and community in fostering resilience. "Connect yourself with the dreamers, the doers, the believers, and thinkers, but most of all, surround yourself with those who see greatness within you, who will be your cheer partner, who will encourage you to move on, but then again you'll have to know that it may not always be that way, connecting is a great way to get that boost forward. To get the encouragement you need to move to the next level. We can never overemphasize the power of connecting with like minds.

After connecting and getting the excitement going, be coachable, teachable, and ready to learn; learn to do what others are doing to succeed, meaning you'll have to put in the work. Life is about everyday learning, but what will be the essence of what you learnt without putting it into action? learn from other people's mistakes, and most importantly, understand the process. The journey of a thousand miles, they say, begins with a step. Start somewhere, be patient, and persevere.

Personal development and commitment to the course are key, and then self-love. If you must overcome challenges, believe in who you are and what you are. Be humble to learn, do not envy or be jealous of anyone because of where you are going in life, set your eyes on your destination, and practice positive affirmations. Tell yourself or call yourself who you want to be, and don't doubt yourself for a second. I remember when I was in high school, I started writing back then as young as that, but when I grew older, I began to ghostwrite books for people. Before I ever wrote a book I could call my own, I was calling myself an author, a speaker, and a philanthropist. in the midst of whatever you may be going through, never walk by what you are seeing or what is happening now, but look up to see your future, beautiful and there comes victory.

Perseverance is often the driving force behind breaking barriers and achieving success. I know so many times it may seem like things are not working, or that you should just throw in the towel. Yes, I understand because I have been there, but I want to encourage you that you can only grow through perseverance; wearing thick skin so you overcome the hurdles of life. I have preserved through difficult seasons in my career and today, I can say, yes, it was worth it.

Create a path and leave your trail: you can't see me on the same path. I bring something new always. If you must achieve something huge and outstanding, learn how to walk alone, rely on yourself, and become your hero. Give the world a reason to admire what you have and who you are.

Our ability to overcome, adapt, and build resilience sets us apart in the face of challenges. Overcoming Challenges and Building Resilience" is to guide us in seeking to break free from the limitations that hold us back. Remember, no barrier is insurmountable when resilience becomes our guiding force.

LOST TIME IS NEVER FOUND AGAIN
LuDrean Peterson

ABOUT THE AUTHOR

LuDrean Howard Peterson, CEO of Delivering on Ideas & Thoughts (DOIT), specializes in turning DREAMERS into DOERS! She's a Human Resources Guru, with 32+ years of experience working in the United States, China, India, South Africa, Latin America, Europe, and Mexico. LuDrean is the host of "Let's Do It" Talk Show and

Visionary-Author of #1 Best-Selling books, *We All Grieve Differently* and *We All Heal Differently,* and a coauthor in six other best-selling anthology projects. She holds dual master's degrees, Master of Business Administration and Master of Science in Management (with an emphasis in HR), and a Master Certification in Project Management. LuDrean is an international speaker, Certified Christian Life Coach, and an international host/emcee. She has two beautiful daughters and three handsome grandsons. LuDrean loves traveling, reading, and engaging in thought-provoking conversations.

Contact LuDrean

- FB: LuDrean Peterson

- IG: @do_it_delivers

- Website: http://www.do-it-delivers.com

- YouTube Channel: Let's Do It Talk Show

CHAPTER 15

Lost Time is Never Found Again

"Lost time is never found again." – Benjamin Franklin

Time lost and wasted can never be recovered or replenished. I've heard, and have used, the phrase "make up for lost time" on numerous occasions. To tell you the truth, it isn't possible to make up for time that has been lost. Time lost is *lost*. It cannot be retrieved nor replaced. Challenges with the management of time are high on the list as a cause for a lot of dreams being deferred. The mismanagement of time shows up in many different forms. One way is giving into the false thinking that multitasking is a skillset (which prevents you from focusing), and then there is the inability to prioritize (which leads you into treating your nice-to-haves the same as your must-haves, and your important tasks the same as your urgent tasks...they are not the same), and we can't leave out procrastination (which convinces you that putting things off will make them disappear...it will not).

"It is impossible to get it done if you don't start." - LuDrean Howard Peterson

Regardless of your "it," you can start doing something to contribute towards reaching a goal you have set. You will never reach your "it" if you never start reaching for "it." As a coach, I help people design and execute plans to help fulfill their dreams. My tagline is "Turning Dreamers into Doers." This is done by taking the first step to spend some time getting your thoughts and ideas out of your head. One of the top reasons provided by most of my clients, as the hindrance of acting towards fulfilling their dreams, is the lack of time. This is not an acceptable answer during my sessions. I explain that we all will dedicate time to do the things that are important to us. Even extremely busy parents, caretakers or businesspeople can do this. Even the smallest amount of time spent on pursuing your dreams, when done repetitively, can help them manifest. Think about how you spend your day, week, or month. It may consist of a combination of work, family responsibilities (taking care of home, children, spouse, parents etc.), eating, sleeping, church, self-care, and social activities. A great percentage of your day-to-day life operates on a recurring cycle. To some degree, this may help you better identify or reallocate time, even if it is a small amount.

For me, balancing motherhood, working, and going to school, simultaneously, was a heavy lift during my undergraduate studies. My "it" was a full plate. I completed most of my homework during my commute on the train to and from work, as well as during my lunch hour. I also dedicated Saturday mornings from 6 am - 9 am to reading and writing papers. My youngest daughter began dance lessons on Saturdays. I studied while in the car waiting for her. By graduate school, I started to get used to my busy schedule. About midway through completion, my school began offering virtual classes. It was such a relief.

It is true that life can be extremely busy for some. However, even the busiest of the busiest can still carve out *some* time for their dreams, even if it is only an hour per month. Remember, you will never reach your "it" if you never start reaching for "it."

"Time is relative; its only worth depends upon what we do as it is passing." - Albert Einstein

This quote is straightforward yet thought provoking. I think the COVID-19 Pandemic led to an increased number of hours people spent on the internet. I get it, we were sheltered-in-place, teleworking full-time and began staying up much later than normal. Social media became our choice of entertainment. It was where we spent many of our hours. We didn't realize the extent until tracking apps were created. Most of the latest phones have apps that track your screen time and how the time spent was allocated. The results were surprising for many, including me! Social media was a tool that I heavily used to promote and stream my videocast. It was a necessity for my business. However, my usage during COVID-19 almost quadrupled the time required. A large portion of my leisure time was squandered on social media. While many people achieved success on social media, it has been dream deferrers or killers for many others. In other words, a lot of time was wasted on social media that could have been better used elsewhere.

I intentionally decided to exchange the hours wasted to spending them on things that better served me. My job became 100% telework during the pandemic and this freed up time that was once spent on getting dressed and commuting. My "Post-Retirement" and "Bucket" Lists included things I wanted to do once I retired. I figured since I had the time, why not get started now. Getting eight hours of sleep, traveling more, spending more time with and helping to care for my grandchildren, returning to school, and teaching were at the top of my list. Dedicating time towards these activities became a natural part of my routine. Traveling became a major part of how I spent a great portion of my time. In 2022, I went on 10 trips, some consisted of week stays and some weekend getaways...some across the globe and some locally...some with family, some with friends and some solo. My grandsons' sports practices, games, tournaments, and activities became a part of my weekly schedule. I graduated from the Nasdaq Entrepreneurial Milestone Circle Program July 2023, created bonds, and spent time with some amazing women entrepreneurs. Also, I completed the requirements to become an Adjunct Trauma Trainer (August 2023) and will complete the requirements to become a Certified Trauma-Competent Professional by the end of 2024.

I strongly encourage you to take some time to reflect on how you are spending and valuing your time. If you find that you are wasting time in areas that do not serve you, then substitute that time with something that does.

"Don't put off until tomorrow what you can do today." — Benjamin Franklin

When your dreams and procrastination clash, it's a zero-sum game. Time spent procrastinating is time lost that could have been spent on your dreams. The more you procrastinate, the farther away you are positioned from fulfilling a dream or completing a task. I can still recall the loud gasp I let out the first time I heard the famous quote by Myles Munroe, who stated, "The graveyard is the richest place on the surface of the earth because there you will see the books never published, ideas that were not harnessed, songs that were not sung and drama pieces that were never acted." The very hard truth in this quote aligns with the basis of my business, Delivering on Ideas and Thoughts (DOIT).

All my life I have been a go-getter. However, turning 50, amid a season of numerous losses of loved ones and a health scare propelled me to reassess how I was spending my time. I remember a conversation with someone who made a statement regarding our age and us probably not having as many years remaining to live as those we have lived thus far. They are probably correct. Truth is, no matter our age, none of us know how long we have left on earth. The transitioning of my three great-great nieces, at the tender ages of 1, 7, and 9, is a daily reminder to me that tomorrow isn't promised.

When you truly understand that once time is lost it can never be found again, it should influence the way you spend your time. I encourage

you to assess your time and start treating time as the priceless commod
ity that it is.

Key Takeaways:

- Lost time is never found again.

- You will never reach your "it" if you never start reaching fo.
"it."

- If you find that you are wasting time in areas that do not serve
you, then substitute that time with something that does.

- Remember, tomorrow is not promised.

GOD HAS EMPOWERED YOU: RELEASE THE WEIGHT AND SOAR!

Kena Smalls

ABOUT THE AUTHOR

Child of GOD, Purpose PusherOwner of Real Time Web Designs & Entrepreneur

During 20 years in government and nonprofit, Kena Smalls developed aspirations of becoming a business owner and entrepreneur. In 2014,

a merger shut down local offices where she worked presenting a prim
opportunity for her to enter the entrepreneurial space.

The early years of business proved to be eye opening, and she quickl
learned business ownership can be a lonely and rocky road. Utilizin
her skills, she began to navigate the online space on behalf of bus
business owners and companies creating websites, brand, assets, busi
ness strategies, providing social media services, and motivating those ir
business.

Understanding and troubleshooting the hurdles businesses sometime
face in their transitional stages became her strong suit. She continue
to count it an honor to support others dreams, purposes, and goals. I
is a part of her ministry, calling, and purpose.

CHAPTER 16

GOD HAS EMPOWERED YOU: RE-LEASE THE WEIGHT AND SOAR!

A love letter to you, my sister...

What does it mean to be "Empowered to Win?" Being empowered is a state that draws on every moment's decision.

Once, I heard someone say that each one of us is an idea of the Most High God. ...Selah... I cannot recall where I heard it, but it stuck to my heart. It changed something in me, and I suggest to you...if each one of us is an idea of the Most High God, then our very essence and life force is the purpose. It is the reason we "are" in the first place.

You Are the Purpose!

What does it mean? It does not necessarily mean isolating yourself and becoming a wanderer. It means the very core of who you are, authentically, as GOD created you, is the purpose to be given to the earth and those on it.

You are the package to be delivered. The purpose makes you feel aliv because it is your breath of life. It connects you to God.

Now, let's talk about the method of delivery.

Being connected to GOD is absolutely essential to planting seeds, wa tering, and rooting yourself in the proper place(s). LOVE is mandatory for the effective delivery of your purpose. Note, many are not accus tomed to seeing authentic purpose flowing free, so you will need some tools to nurture, protect, and nourish yourself.

Nurture - Stay connected, lean on, depend, believe, trust in and or GOD for He is the source.

Protect - When tested, stand on your commitment, resilience, GOD's Word to you, His strength, and guidance.

Nourish - Release negative people, places, and things. Love on yourself as you do others, remain flexible, and allow growth.

Walking In Purpose

You have an invitation, a birthright, to life being one with your pur pose in GOD. Walking in your purpose is an **Intimate Act of Love towards the Father**.

The Journey Back to Your Truth

Do not try to shape GOD into the God you prefer Him to be. Allow Him to bless you with the life He has created you for.

Shedding the Weight

Let's talk about shedding the weight between you and your purpose. Many find themselves, like a distant shore staring off at their purpose, a.k.a your true self, trying to find their path home. Burdened with the fear of social judgment and discomfort, we carry weight like a ton of bricks, dragging behind us. Begin shedding the weight of:

Habits: Reflect on Romans 7:15-20. Paul talked about overcoming the flesh. Put away the bad habits that keep you from your purpose. It is easier said than done but must be accomplished on your journey to God's best for you.

People: People do not stop us, but we do stop ourselves because of the thoughts, impressions, and opinions of others. For this, I say, one day we will stand before God. Will your reasons for not walking in your purpose be enough to satisfy God?

Circumstances: God will never place you out of His reach so we must walk in faith. He knows exactly what you contend with and the path to freedom. Trust, believe, persist, and actively move towards God in ALL your ways, no matter what it looks like.

Limitations: The truth is, there is no limitation that will keep you from God's call on your life. He knows every temporary setback you face and will ever face along with every lesson. We have an all-knowing loving father, who would not call you to do something he knows you cannot do. Period.

Build The Bridge by Breaking Down Fear

"Your best life is on the other side of fear." ~Will Smith's Grandmother~

There is nothing between you and your purpose, but the dense energy of fear. Fear is a deceptive and cunning tool used by many... the enemy, our thoughts, friends, loved ones, and more. Most use it with the best intentions but they do not know God's plan for you. He is the orchestrator of this symphony, and his plan is, hands-down, the best plan for you no matter what anyone else thinks. So, how do we build the bridge through our fears?

Be Afraid and Do It Anyway

If God is calling you into the storm, be afraid, if you must, but do it anyway. If God is calling you to the top of a mountain and your family and friends are telling you of all the dangers, trust in God and do it anyway.

148

With all this being said, trusting God stands on the fact that you are connected and hearing from God. Maintain a strong devotional life. Go to God as a child because He cares about absolutely everything that is going on with you. Take your fears, emotions, strengths, weaknesses, uprisings, and downfalls all to God for repair, revelation, renewal, and restoration. He is 100% faithful.

Try this task to unmask fear:

Say out loud a belief or statement you believe is stopping you from living your purposed life.

Then ask, "why?"

Once you answer, ask "why?" again.

Continue to ask "why?" until you reach the core of that belief.

This will help you see what is fueling your disbelief and if it is, indeed, fear at the core.

In closing, my sister, please remember **you are an idea of the Most High God, purpose in the flesh** created by the absolute best. There is nothing that can separate you from your purpose, it is who you are. God wrapped your earthly flesh around a purpose. It's called [SAY YOUR NAME HERE].

Walk in your birthright. Walk in your purpose. There is where you will find authenticity, joy, happiness, and more...but most importantly, intimate communion with the Most High God, through the power of Jesus Christ, our Lord and Savior.

Again, I say, SOAR!!! God empowered you the moment He spoke your beautiful name!

Love, your sis, Kena!

Journey of a Fearless Mompreneur: A Story of Empowerment and Growth
Dr. Daphne Soares

ABOUT THE AUTHOR

Dr. Daphne Soares, the Founder of Carousel Moms Business and Leadership Coaching, is an accomplished individual with numerous accolades and honorary doctorates. She has been recognized as the

Gold First Place Winner - 'Coach of the Year 2023' by Women Changing the World in London, the Top Business Coach by The NYC Journal, and ranked among the Top 10 Female Coaches by Yahoo Finance. With a portfolio of 13x international bestselling books, including a collaboration with Les Brown, Dr. Soares is a respected authority in her field.

As an internationally certified Business and Leadership Coach, counselor, motivational speaker, and mentor, Dr. Soares is devoted to empowering women worldwide through personalized coaching sessions conducted online and in-person. She guides women in confidently stepping into entrepreneurship, attaining financial freedom, and making a lasting impact. Driven by her expertise and unwavering support, she equips individuals with the tools and guidance needed to succeed and unlock their full potential.

CHAPTER 17

JOURNEY OF A FEARLESS MOMPRE- NEUR: A STORY OF EMPOWERMENT AND GROWTH

The decision to establish Carousel Moms Business and Leadership Coaching marked a pivotal turning point in my life, a moment of profound significance that shaped my journey towards purpose and fulfillment. It was the culmination of my unwavering passion for helping others and my deep-seated yearning to venture into the world of entrepreneurship. The prospect of building a coaching business that would empower and uplift moms globally filled me with enthusiasm and excitement, yet it also cast shadows of doubt and fear over the path that lay ahead.

As I reflect on the early days of my coaching journey, I am reminded of the mix of emotions that consumed me. The idea of creating a business where I could combine my desire to assist others with my entrepreneurial dreams was invigorating. Still, the uncertainty and fear of failure lingered, casting doubts on my abilities and the viability of my aspirations. Yet, deep within my heart, there was an undeniable calling, a voice urging me to move forward, to take that leap of faith into the unknown.

Transitioning from exclusively a counselor to a business and leadership coach, while drawing on my counseling expertise, revealed to me the life-changing potential of embracing fear and turning my dreams into reality. Initially, the fear of failure held me back, fueling doubts and insecurities. However, acknowledging these fears became the catalyst for my personal growth. Each mistake and setback turned into a valuable learning experience, propelling me to take calculated risks and venture outside my comfort zone. It was through this process that I came to realize that fear could be a potent driving force, urging me onward rather than hindering my progress.

The days leading up to the launch of Carousel Moms were filled with both trepidation and excitement. There were moments when self-doubt threatened to overpower my resolve, but deep down, I knew that my passion and unwavering belief in the value of my services would guide me through any adversity that may arise.

Running Carousel Moms and being a devoted mom demanded a delicate balancing act. I learned the art of meticulous planning, setting clear boundaries, and effective communication with my family to ensure that both aspects of my life harmoniously coexisted. This integration became a journey of self-discovery, wherein I found immense fulfillment in nurturing both my family and my entrepreneurial pursuits.

As I began one-on-one personalized and group coaching sessions with my clients, I felt a profound sense of responsibility and gratitude. These brave women had entrusted me with their dreams, their struggles, and their desire for positive change. With each coaching session, I witnessed the transformative power of encouragement, support, and belief. As they made strides towards their goals, I, too, grew as a coach, learning to adapt my strategies, develop my intuition, and celebrate their victories as if they were my own.

Guidance from seasoned entrepreneurs played a pivotal role in my development as a mompreneur. Embracing the concept of "standing on the shoulders of giants," I sought wisdom and inspiration from those who had triumphed before me. Their insights not only boosted my confidence but also provided invaluable guidance in navigating the challenges of entrepreneurship.

Defining my vision and identifying my coaching niche brought clarity and purpose to my journey. Understanding my passions and unique skill set allowed me to effectively target the audience I sought to serve. Armed with a clear sense of purpose, I persevered even during the toughest times, knowing that my efforts were making a positive impact on the lives of others.

Confidence became a cornerstone of my journey as a mompreneur. Drawing upon the confidence of influential figures like Tony Robbins, John Maxwell, John Mattone, Mel Robbins, Grant Cardone, Les Brown, and others bolstered my self-assurance. Surrounding myself with supportive and like-minded individuals helped me confront my fears of failure, rejection, and criticism with unwavering resolve. Their encouragement and validation empowered me to showcase my skills and expertise with newfound confidence.

Embracing the fear of failure and treating mistakes as stepping stones to personal growth revolutionized my mindset. Adopting a growth-oriented approach, I learned to leverage setbacks as opportunities for improvement. This transformation allowed me to rebound stronger after every challenge, embracing new obstacles with courage. I realized that mistakes were an integral part of the learning process and did not define my worth or abilities. Instead, failure became a signal to explore new paths rather than a dead-end.

With my coaching business flourishing, my primary focus shifted towards empowering women globally. My mission was to instill self-confidence, foster personal growth, promote financial freedom, and nurture a culture of success among my clients. This dedication to my clients' success and satisfaction became the driving force behind my pursuit of excellence.

Engaging with like-minded individuals became transformative, offering valuable exchanges of knowledge and insights. This sense of camaraderie within the entrepreneurial community enriched my journey as a mompreneur. As I balanced my family life with my business pursuits, leveraging my expertise as a counselor and NLP Master Practitioner, I found unparalleled fulfillment. Guiding my children to understand the values of resilience, dedication, and the pursuit of passion reinforced my own determination to excel in both roles - as a nurturing mother and a thriving business owner.

Over the years, my coaching journey has been marked by numerous accolades and global recognition. In 2021, Yahoo Finance honored me by listing me among the Top 10 International Female Coaches, while The NYC Journal featured me as one of the Top 30 Business Coaches in 2022. The pinnacle of my achievements came in 2023 when Women Changing the World bestowed upon me the prestigious title of 'Coach of the Year,' along with first-place gold winner recognition and numerous other international accolades. These acknowledgments served as a powerful affirmation of the effectiveness and impact of my coaching services and inspired me to reach even greater heights in empowering women globally to embrace their potential and flourish.

The decision to establish Carousel Moms Business and Leadership Coaching was not merely about building a business; it was an act of courage and determination to make a difference in the lives of others and empowering them to win in their carousel of life. Living a life of choice and on purpose. Thus creating a legacy. It was a journey of self-discovery, finding harmony between my passion for helping others and my pursuit of entrepreneurship. Balancing the roles of a mompreneur was not without its challenges, but through resilience, unwavering belief, and the support of my loved ones, I emerged stronger and more committed than ever to empowering moms and fostering leadership in women worldwide. As I continue on this transformative path, I am driven by a sense of purpose, a passion for growth, and an unwavering commitment to making a positive impact on the lives of others through Carousel Moms Business and Leadership Coaching.

Think to Win: You Have the Power!

Mireille Toulekima

ABOUT THE AUTHOR

Mireille Toulekima is a multi-talented woman whose versatility and accomplishments across diverse disciplines have earned her global recognition. She is a Public Figure, Award-Winning Engineer, and entrepreneur who gained experience working in Africa, Europe, Asia, and

Australia. Her global touch is visible in related endeavors she actively engages in.

Mireille is also the executive producer and host of the global talk show, "The Greatness Engineering Hour." She consistently motivates and empowers individuals. Her dedication to helping others achieve greatness is truly inspiring. She is part of the class of women who have embraced non-traditional industries, philanthropy, spiritual consciousness, and mindfulness.

CHAPTER 18

THINK TO WIN: YOU HAVE THE POWER!

We live in a volatile, uncertain, complex, and challenging world. It is often difficult to believe that we can be successful and win in such an environment. Yet it is during the most difficult times in life that we must refuse to accept whatever comes our way. We must remind ourselves that we were born to win and were created to be champions in life. We are powerful beyond measure. We must step into our unique power whenever things get tough. We must think to win!

Problems and challenges will always be part of life. We all have problems and concerns. The real perspective we should adopt is that our problems and concerns are temporary and understand that God is bigger than any problems any of us have.

When I started working in the male-dominated oil and gas industry, instead of taking pride in being the 1st black woman petroleum engineer of my country of origin (Gabon) working for a multinational, I instead saw myself as different and lacking the required skills to make it in this industry. I already had all the excuses to justify my failure. I saw myself as an imposter and not good enough to compete with my male counterparts and make it in the oil and gas industry. I was focusing on all the negatives and what I was lacking instead of building myself up from what I had accomplished.

Negative thoughts and emotions can overwhelm us and rob us of perspective. If we do not shut them down, self-destruction can seem like the only escape because we cannot see another way out! When we feel overwhelmed by negative emotions, it is important to have faith, look at the big picture, and understand that if we are living and breathing there is always a possibility of better days ahead, and there is always an opportunity to get out of our comfort zone and push ourselves to win despite the fear and perceived shortcomings.

Fear of the unknown leaves many of us stagnating. We are frightened to take the plunge and risks necessary even when we know that the results will make us a winner. We forget that the challenges that we go through are key to our growth and improvements in every aspect of our life.

However, one thing that is real is that we all can become visionaries. We all have a story we tell ourselves about how we want the future to be. Thinking to win demands that we have a goal on which to focus. If we fasten our attention to what we already know, then we will only repeat the present in the future and experience no growth. The first step to winning is to focus on where we wish to be or what we want to attain. For this, we need a personal vision and specific goals. Once we have our vision and set our goals, we are ready to focus on immediate plans.

Whatever our vision, we will have inner and outside resources to help achieve it and inner and outside obstacles in our path. Be prepared!

Our personal vision is our guide to a winning future. It helps us to choose a path through the infinite possibilities of life. It helps us to find our way around obstacles, cut through the undergrowth of life, and provides trail marks and signposts to keep us on track. It is an acknowledgment of our own unique potential and the power we must create in the life of a winner. A shift happened later in my career because I understood the value of building on my faith and having a personal vision. Winning was now an integral part of my life because I realized that I had to clearly embody my vision. It was not enough to know how I want to be and have, I also needed to think to win, be able to feel and experience being that way with all my senses: seeing, hearing, feeling, even conjuring up my sensations.

It is essential to bear in mind that our personal visions are dynamic. Everything changes. With time some aspects of our personal vision will change. As we grow and develop and begin to embody it, we will discover things about ourselves that we do not know yet. New goals and aspirations will emerge. Further horizons may present themselves. We must always be alert to new opportunities. Be open to them when they arise. So, the best way to create opportunities and win in the future is to get on with putting our vision into action. At each step of the way we must remember what Zig Ziglar said: "You were born to win but to be a winner, you must plan to win, prepare to win, and expect to win." It is an ongoing process. The keys to sustainable winning are self-belief, readiness, and persistence. We must be tenaciously and ruthlessly persistent. There will be all sorts of barriers and obstacles we will have to overcome if we want to achieve our dreams. Dreams do not just roll over and die. We must go for them and never give up.

As I have worked globally through the years with people who have achieved much and have lives that are constantly in high gear, I noticed that they are people with an extraordinary ability to know the right thing to do and to do it in a timely fashion. They are also people who place a high emphasis on and strive for excellence in every area of life. To win it is important to become a person of

vision, passion, priority, and excellence. To empower ourselves to win we must:

1. Have a vision for our lives

2. Fuel our passion and work hard enough to get the right results

3. Adopt the right mindset

4. have a positive mental attitude building on challenges and obstacles we faced

In the end, the measure of our success comes down to who wins the battle that rages between the two of us. The "us" who wants to stop, give up, or take it easy, and the "us" who chooses to beat that which would stand in the way of our dreams. We choose: lose or win!!

THE MESS THAT BECAME A MIRACLE!

Dr. Canzada Twyman

ABOUT THE AUTHOR

Dr. Canzada Twyman is an authentic, anointed woman of God, in love with the Lord. She is joyfully married to one man, a mother, grand and great-grand mother: a loyal family member and friend to many. She is the FEO of the Divine Exchange Ministry, Inc., (DEMI). Dr. Canzada is a learned woman who has obtained a Doctorate in Religious Philosophy, MHS, and a BS. She is a National and International Training Provider for DEMI Training, Collaboration & Consulting Services. This trailblazer is a U. S. Army Veteran, a humanitarian, visionary, a published and contributing author. Being flexible and operating in many roles, she is an inspirational, motivational public speaker, an ordained Pastor, Prophetic Intercessor, and Spiritual Life Coach.

CHAPTER 19

THE MESS THAT BECAME A MIRACLE!

It's like the runaway child, I became so, so wild. Coming back home from the military and living a life within a controlled environment, I really didn't know what to do. That military experience and all the trauma, the hurt, and pain, the disappointment, the anger, bitterness and yes resentment actually dictated my life for over twenty-seven years. I was a mess, when I think about the abuse endured in the military and within unhealthy relationships, and just not knowing where to turn I'm forever grateful today. When I reflect back on the mess, I declare it was indeed a mess in which I'm not proud of, but not ashamed of it either. One may say, well what is the mess? First allow me to break down that word 'mess,' which is defined as dirty, disorder, and disarray. The mess is just an unpleasant, untidy situation to live within, that thing manifests and destroys behaviors, mind-sets, relationships, and even families. The mess breaths disorganization, discouragement, and even despair. There go I... yes, I was a total MESS. My house, my temple was messy and after twenty-seven years of running from me, I made a sound decision to clean the house.

I present a question to all the readers... Do you need to clean your house? You do know that your body is the temple that holds the wholeness, wellness, and the wealth of life and when we don't keep it clean and allow the Power greater than self to rise, then the temple, your house, my house becomes messy. My house was messy, a total mess, a cluttered mind-set, with a dirty heart, which led me to misconduct and undesirable behaviors. It's just like the story in bible located in Matthew 7, Jesus said, "everyone who hears His words and **puts them into practice** *is like a wise person who built their house on the rock.* Then He went on to say everyone who hears His words and **does not put them into practice** *is like a foolish person who built their house on sand.*" (Matthew 7:24-26). I built my house on sinking sand, which was a false foundation that left me empty, in shambles, struggling with negative thoughts, behaviors, and people; it was the only ground upon which I demonstrated. I was foolish, uncertain regarding life, and I just desired a change.

Listen, I would work every day and would leave work to go to my part-time job, I was a professional theft-entrepreneur, not a drug store bandit. It was my part-time job and I worked it daily, 4 to 5 hours every evening and I must say the pay was really good back then. The stealing, robbing, drug selling and using; the criminal thinking and the street mentality became a lifestyle for me. I often tell people I received a Ph.D. in Street-ology, because I earned that degree from the negative lifestyle. You do know that everything is permissible, but not everything is beneficial. The slick talking, fly dressing fellows, the clothes, money, jewelry, nice cars, the entertainment, drinks, and drugs all those things are indeed permissible, but I declare they were not beneficial for me, and it all captured me for a long, long time. I was a hostage and didn't have sense enough to know that I was being held hostage. Didn't realize that it all was a major distraction. Listen, the enemy will really dress it up and present a smoke screen to make it all look so EASY. Understand, great people when the enemy makes it EASY and you really don't know any better, unable to step up and out of the smoke screen, and the deception is rooted... that part right there leads to self-deception, which alters a sense of self and sense of reality. I was right there; my cognitive thinking was distorted, and emotions were damaged; and when this happens to a person the Power greater than self must intervene. An intervention that is NOT explicable by natural or scientific laws. I needed an AUTHENTIC MIRACLE!

It was in Brooklyn, N.Y. after receiving a major breakthrough from a suicidal attempt, I received this phenomenon supernatural Divine Exchange in my life. Yes, a miracle took place and it was not EASY. I believe in miracles, and I believe in angels for I've experienced a supernatural miracle and I've been in the very presence of angels. This intervention took place in a laundry room as I sat for ninety days, reading the Bible and studying the book of Deuteronomy; crying out to the God of my understanding, weeping to God Almighty, in which I could not see; but hear me when I say I felt a soft wind and an overwhelming presence in that laundry room. I heard a soft voice say, *"follow me my daughter, I am with you, just follow me."* I didn't know at the time that it was the presence and voice of God. Yes, during that ninety-day period I received visitations from the Lord, not realizing that He was performing a miracle. He was conducting a Divine Exchange within me.

That word miracle is an extraordinary event that surpasses all known human and or natural powers; it is indeed a wonder. I realize today that it's only God, my old nature had to die in order for the newness of life to be resurrected. It is a miracle, for many years I believed what was told to me, you are going to be just like your mother, you will never be anything in life. A treatment doctor told me that you will always be on methadone and more than likely you will die on it. Well please know that the devil is indeed a liar straight from the pits of hell and the truth is nowhere in him. I'm living evidence that the all-knowing, powerful, and great God is ready, willing, and able to do exceedingly and abundantly above all you or I could ask or even think; research it in Ephesians 3:20.

Yes, my life was a total mess and daily I would rise, go work and do what I needed to do, but when I yielded in the laundry room, became vulnerable, and made that sound decision, the Miracle took place. When my ninety days of discipline was up and I stepped back in position the Glory of God was upon, among, and within me. I'm evidence that God is Able to perform Miracles, He did it with Moses, Mary, Paul, Lazarus, and many more He will do it for you.

Great People, know that you deserve to win, the Power of God can and will Empower You to Win... but you must allow Him to do so. I had to allow the Power of God to take charge, I removed myself from the driver's seat and allowed Him to be the driver and I just follow. I had to allow Him to build my esteem, confront my damaged emotions, step up and out of fear, manage my anger, and most of all, obtain deliverance from self. Yes, I had to be delivered from self. I was my worst enemy, oh but today my beloved I WIN... I'm Empowered to Win, and so are you. Understand that the enemy fights those who know exactly *Who they are, and Whose they are.* The Greater the assignment the more the enemy will fight; oh, but hear me when I say, God will Empower you with His wisdom, knowledge, fearlessness, boldness, and His Greatness to Win.

Love Always Wins
Claudia Newby-Tynes

About the Author

"The ministry is His...I am His pen," says Claudia Newby-Tynes, who serves as Kingdom Communicator/Scribe in the Kingdom for such as time as this. As entrepreneur behind Write 4U, Claudia is an author, teacher/preacher, and mentor. She answered "Yes" to God's call to ministry. She is passionate about fulfilling His call and purpose as a daughter of the King. Her greatest joy comes in doing Kingdom business for her (Abba) Father.

Claudia travels and presents (in-person and virtually) at conferences, workshops, and book signings. Claudia shares her literary works via television, radio, podcasts, social media, and blogs interviews. She has penned four books, collaborated on two book projects; and freelanced over 225+ published clips online and in print media.

Claudia and her family live in Smithfield, Virginia. She and her husband, James, celebrate 52 years of marriage, and they have one adult son, Rodney. Claudia and James are members at Soteria Life Center under the leadership of Pastors Perry and Dr. Belinda Moss,

"I came to serve. My duty is to serve. In order to be like Jesus, I must serve."

To learn more visit **http://claudiatynes.com**

CHAPTER 20

LOVE ALWAYS WINS

Beloved, you have everything you need to win; it's God-given and it's within you. You are the purpose, you are powerful, and winning is your portion. Allow God to exchange all the mess and perform a miracle in you! Be Empowered to Win.

Women are responders. We are emergency responders (EMTs), military veterans, doctors and nurses, and the lists are endless. In each profession, women are always on call and ready to respond to whatever situation we are called to respond. Throughout history, women were pioneers and trailblazers in all walks of life. As a woman believer, a general theme came to my mind, "Love." Love is an action word because love gives. Love is God, for God so loved the world, He gave. Women, by nature, are responders and nurturers. We are receivers and givers. Women are always on the call of duty 24/7 because of the love and compassion we possess helping and caring for others. As women, we aim to win, not just to win but win triumphantly. Why? Because God has already empowered us to win.

Here are four (4) points for you to ponder:

1. Women: Responding to the Call of Duty to Love (*Matthew 22:37-38*) *"Thou shalt love the Lord thy God with ALL of thy heart, and with ALL of thy soul, and with ALL of thy mind. This is the first and great commandment."*

Our first response to the call of duty is to love our God with every fiber of our total being: spirit, soul and body. For it is in Him; we live, we move, and we have our being. Without Him, we are nothing; but in Him we are complete. We can do ALL things because He infuses us with His love and His strength.

2. Women: Call to Duty to Love thy Neighbor as Thysel (*Matthew 22:39-40*) *"And the second is like unto it, "Thou shalt love thy neighbor as thyself. On these two commandments hang ALL the law and the prophets."*

One scripture asks the question, "How can you love God who you have not seen, and hate your brother who you have seen?" Obviously, this was a rebuke from God. We cannot give out what we do not have. God is full of compassion (love); He met the people where they were (are). Who is your neighbor? Your neighbor is everyone who God has placed in your sphere of influence. If we as women, are imitators of our God, we cannot pick and choose who to love. We are instructed to love our enemies Now, that's a hard task - you can only love your enemies with the love of God. First of all, we must love ourselves; then that same love of God that is in our hearts is spread abroad to others by the Holy Ghost.

. Women: Call to Duty for the Love of Family *(Proverbs 1(27-28), "She looketh well to the ways of her household, and eateth ot the bread of idleness. Her children arise up, and call her blessed; her usband also, and he praiseth her."* Charity (love) starts at home, then it s spread abroad. One of the highest callings of women is motherhood. Her first ministry is to her family. The "Proverbs 31 Woman" is the perfect example of a woman called to duty in every aspect of life. She knew who and whose she was in Christ. As a result, she responded to life situations with Godly character; she feared (reverenced) the Lord. Titus 2 (3-5) is another good example of women called to duty for the ove of family. Please read and meditate during your private devotions.

. Women: Call to Duty for the Love of Ministry *(Galatians 5:13-14), "For brethren (that includes women too), ye have been called unto liberty; only use not liberty for an occasion to the flesh, but by love erve one another. For all the law is fulfilled in one word, even in this, "Thou shalt love thy neighbor as thyself."*

So what does ministry mean to you? Is ministry having a world-wide traveling teaching/preaching ministry? Is ministry standing in the pulpit declaring the Word of God? Is ministry helping the homeless with food, shelter, and clothing? Is ministry caring for the sick? Is ministry being a stay-at-home mom? *Ministry is all of the above, plus more.* Simply put, ministry is serving. Our Lord is the greatest of ALL Servants. He is our Master; and no servant is greater than His master. If Jesus came to serve (and He did); we as women who are the called according to His will and His purpose are also called to duty for the love of ministry (serving). We are servers for the Kingdom of God.

Listen Up God's Women:

We are called to duty to:

(1) Love God first and foremost.

(2) Love our neighbors as we do ourselves.

(3) Love our families.

(4) Love to minister (serving and loving God's people wherever we find them). God has empowered you and me. He designed each one of us wonderfully and fearfully on purpose for a purpose. We are different by design, on purpose, for a purpose. So go forth in your calling knowing God has got you in the palm of His hands! We WIN. We are WINNERS because Jesus always causes us to TRIUMPH in Him! To God be all the Glory!

MINDSET AND PERMISSION
C. Tina Wall

ABOUT THE AUTHOR

C. Tina Wall is a motivator, organizer, entrepreneur, and writer. Tina was born and raised in the nation's capital, Washington, D.C., she now lives with her family in Maryland. Although Tina worked in several areas such as the school system, the private sector, and later the federal government, she knew that her calling was bigger than those 9-5 opportunities. Tina loves meeting new people, traveling, and spending time with her family and friends. Also in her spare time, she finds time to work on her first motivational book. Tina has a strong desire to change the mindset of the masses.

CHAPTER 21

MINDSET AND PERMISSION

To my sisters, ask yourself a few questions: "What am I here for?" "What am I supposed to do with my life?" "What is my purpose and how do I get there?" These are personal questions that I asked myself for many years until I started listening and looking at life differently. My journey took a long while to start because I had no idea that life was not always about just going to work, paying bills, and living a mediocre lifestyle. Before I continue, understand that I knew that I was blessed throughout my life, but there had to be something more in me and in life. I had no idea that the things that I was doing without effort were my gifts and talents. Then I started getting ideas of owning and running businesses, thoughts of writing a book and speaking on stages. But the big question remained, where do I start? Because I didn't have a business background or the blueprint to do this on my own, I started doing research, printing, and reading everything that I could to jump start my journey. I made notebooks for all of my ideas, but I was still stuck. One day as I was listening to the radio, I heard something about an "act like a success conference." So, without hesitation, I made the decision to attend the weekend event. This was the beginning of one of the best decisions that I ever made. I witnessed platforms that planted seeds and changed my mindset forever. This conference left me hungry for success. This led me to researching and printing even more information. But this time, the information was different, my thinking was different, and my attitude changed. Now I had to win! I knew that success was not overnight and there is a road to travel. Many times, we wait for others to tell us what to do and how to move because that is what we are used to. Why? For many of us, we won't move until we are told to do so. Now that you have identified this, stop! When you give yourself permission, you are changing your mindset. Get uncomfortable and start right where you are now. We all have ideas, gifts, and talents to share that the world needs. Do not be afraid to duplicate and master your gifts. Find some mentors, but understand this, you cannot do this alone.

When I started thinking differently, I started moving differently. I put down the romance novels and started reading self-developing and em-powering books. Now this didn't happen overnight, but eventually, I did it. Confession: I still have a few novels that I held onto but haven't picked them up in many years. I stopped watching television as much and discovered YouTube. I discovered that listening and watching motivating material feeds and encourages me a little bit more each time to be very beneficial. I find that we cannot continue to be our own and worst critic or our own enemy. We can and have caused our own sabotage and downfall. Take the leap of faith today and give yourself a chance to become a better version of yourself. You owe you. In the process, know that everyone will not be excited about you or support you. Build up your faith muscle, limit distractions and know that life will be living everyday whether you want it to or not. We cannot control every aspect of our lives. But imagine what it could look like if you try or what would it look like if you don't try? Make a decision.

The push is internal, so that means that it starts within and the road that you must take is specifically designed for you. This is your path. Now get up, brush yourself off and put one foot in front of the other. Most people are worried about the masses of people that will not support them. So what! Remember that these are your dreams, visions, and your goals alone. God never shares these with other people. Their permission and opinion of you should never matter. Develop your drive, tenacity, focus, self-worth, build character and commitment to your success habits. I hear over and over again to stop telling your big dreams to small-minded people. You know why? Because they will kill them every time.

Funny Story

I had an executive that was new to the office, and he wanted to get to know the staff. So, he walked the halls until one day, it was my turn for his visit. As we chatted, he asked me about my goals and dreams. I was super excited and thought to myself, I feel confident enough to share. No harm, no foul. Right? Nope, wrong. So, I proceeded to share my ideas and this joker shot down each one of them, one by one. So, I was like wait, what is happening?! Me being me, a little sassy sometimes, but I had a comeback for him to match the smug look on my face. I only shared two (2) of my dream goals because I didn't like what he was doing. Immediately, everything in me told me that this joker was trying to discourage me with everything he had in him. Guess what? It didn't work, I changed the subject, ended our conversation to match my stare, my smug look and resumed working. He eventually got the message and left my office. When he was out the door, I laughed and labeled him a "dream killer." After that visit, our conversations were only work-related and very limited. In short, don't allow others to dictate your future or deter you to make you second guess yourself. Look at dream killers as fuel to your fire and as motivation.

Make the decision to give it all you got.

Believe in yourself because I believe in you, too.

Success comes with failure, fail forward.

Make it make sense.

DELIGHT YOURSELF IN THE LORD AND HE WILL GIVE YOU YOUR HEART'S DESIRES

Evangelist Bertha D. Winston

ABOUT THE AUTHOR

Evangelist Bertha D. Winston was born in Franklin, Virginia, and was raised in Jackson, North Carolina. She and her husband have been married to each other for 53 years. She is the mother of three, one son and two daughters, seven grandchildren and four great grandchildren. She is an entrepreneur, co-owner of the Pavilion Exclusive Event and Conference Center; owner of Destined2Millions and The Winston Experience where she teaches personal financial success via strategies.

Evangelist Bertha Winston has been a member of Jesus Way Temple Christian Church for 40 plus years. She serves as Secretary, Board Member, Worship Leader, and Associate Minister. Also, she is a Board Member for the foreign missions in the Republic of Haiti. She served as Board Member and several other offices for the National Network for Christian Men and Women. Currently, she is the Office Manager for a prestigious law firm in the DMV metropolitan area and she is co-author of two anthologies, with AGD Publishing Company out of Maryland.

Bertha Winston has developed an exemplary professional career. Her desire is to educate and inspire women to become more knowledgeable about their financial freedom through Destined2Millions and The Winston Experience. She was a radio personality for eight years on the 1340 AM WYCB Radio Station, hosting the Eagle Kind Radio Broadcast.

Evangelist Winston lives in the DMV area, District Heights, Maryland.

CHAPTER 22

DELIGHT YOURSELF IN THE LORD AND HE WILL GIVE YOU YOUR HEART'S DESIRES

At age 60, I wanted to celebrate my birthday in Paris. My Goddaughter was stationed in Germany at the time. Her mother and I have been friends for 30 plus years. I was one of the bride's maids at her wedding. Both my Goddaughter, her sister and I flew to Germany to visit her daughter. Her daughter took the week off and drove us to Paris. We spent two nights there. It was one of the best birthdays I had ever experienced. I was so excited that God allowed my wish to come true to be in Paris on my 60th birthday. We also visited Belgium and did a lot of touring. What a wonderful experience! I have also traveled to Trinidad, West Indies, the Republic of Haiti, and The Bahamas.

After returning to work after the breast surgery the school system had a Reduction in Force (RIF), but the good news was that they would have to place you in another position. Although I was told that they did not have another position for me and that I would probably be without a job beginning June 2008, I told them you do not know the

God I serve! I know and I believe He will make sure I have a job by the end of June 2008. At the end of June 2008, I was called into the Office of the Board of Education, and I was told that she had some bad news and some good news. She asked me *which one do you want to hear first*? I replied that *it really does not matter*. She said you do have a job, but you will be transferred to a school in Beltsville, Maryland. I was not happy about the commute, but I trusted God that I would have a job by the end of June 2008, and He made it happen. The rule was that if you get riffed from your job you are supposed to be placed in a position not more than a 10-mile radius from where you currently worked. That did not happen, but God made sure I had a job. He did not let me down; I was simply not happy to be placed back in a school setting again. I really hated the job, and I prayed every day for God to deliver me from this job, because I knew and God knew, that working in the school arena was not my calling. But, nevertheless, I worked as if I loved the job and no one at the job knew that I could not stand working at that school. I kept telling the other secretary that God was going to deliver me from this job and give me a better job that I really liked. Well, my girlfriend discovered a lawyer she knew who was looking for a legal secretary. I had not been working in the legal field for about 15 plus years, but I sent in my resume anyway. I was interviewed for the position of Secretary/Office Manager. I said to the Lord, "*God, are You sure*"? Now mind you, as I said previously, I had not worked in the legal field for 15 plus years, but I was offered the position and I accepted it and have been working for my boss for 14 plus years now.

I love my job, I worked hard, and it is the highest paying job I have ever held and the best boss one could ever ask for and I am extremely happy to say that this year 2023, at age 72, I will be retiring from this very prestigious law firm in downtown District of Columbia. What a journey I have been on, and again to God be All the Glory!

THE STRENGTH TO SOAR
Allison G. Daniels

ABOUT THE AUTHOR

Allison G. Daniels is as an awarding-winning, 18-time best-selling author who has written over 31 books and a Life Coach, Allison Daniels is extremely honored and blessed to help empower women in various stages of their lives and to those who are seeking professional and personal growth through venues that provide motivation, awareness, and mentoring. Allison is a Multi-Visionary Author of the Book Series *"Empowered to Win, Unshakable Faith* and *Women Be Free.*

Allison teaches life skills to women in the form of discipleship, stewardship and servant leadership via networking, teaching, mentoring, workshops, conferences, and the like. Allison is the owner of Allison Daniels Ministries, LLC; Founder/CEO of the "Write 2 Finish Now! Book Program," where she teaches writers how to write their books and share their stories. She is the Founder/CEO of AGD Publishing Services, where it is her mission to turn writers into successful authors --one book at a time.

She is the Founder/CEO of Women Empowered 2 Win Organization, which is geared to empower and educate women of all ages to lead with authority. She is an accomplished Author, Speaker, Coach, and Licensed Minister. Also, Allison has a Monday Morning Facebook Live @ 5am Segment, and she is a former Co-host of the WBGR radio show, "LetsDoThis" and former Podcast Host of "Gospel Time Machine." She is the host of two (2) podcasts: *Authors Chat with Allison* and *The Authors Lab.* She uses her books, coaching and her mentoring skills as tools to help and assist those who are ready to lead with authority, lead with clarity and lead with confidence toward their next level up. Her mission is to aspire, dream and motivate others.

CHAPTER 23

THE STRENGTH TO SOAR

"But those who wait for the Lord [who expect, look for, and hope in Him] shall change *and* renew their strength *and* power; they shall lift their wings *and* mount up [close to God] as eagles [mount up to the sun]; they shall run and not be weary, they shall walk and not faint *or* become tired." Isaiah 40:31 Amplified Bible, Classic Edition (AMPC)

Every day I had to pray for the strength to soar. I had to pray for the strength to be able to move in power and in peace. I had to begin to encourage myself and unload my emotional baggage and step out of my comfort zone and allow God to heal me from the inside out. I was going through a time in my life where I didn't feel like I had the strength to keep pressing on. I had a lot of responsibilities and obligations that I needed to complete and accomplish but I was drained from my daily tasks.

I knew that I had a lot on my plate being a caregiver for both my parents and running a publishing business. But I had a lot of unanswered questions and visions and dreams that I wanted to fulfill. So, I had to wait for God's Word before I moved forward to executive my business or to write another book. My entire goal was to build my life around the Word of God so that I can soar in His strength and His goals for my life.

I started keeping a daily journal to help me with releasing some of my daily anxieties, disappointments, achievements, and goals. Writing in my journal each day gave me an opportunity to share my private thoughts and your private emotions with the Lord.

I really learned how to develop a consistent prayer life and relying on the Lord. I started being intentional about needing the strength of the Lord for me to soar that I began to change the way that I was thinking. I began to develop a positive mindset daily. I knew that I needed to renew my mind. I need to transform my thought life and begin to process and view things the way that God sees it. I needed to align my thought life up with God. Romans 12: says "you should not conform to the world but be transformed by the renewing of your mind."

I truly wanted to create my own destiny as to how I wanted to live the rest of my life and be quick to adapt to a positive change before the change changed me. I wrote down a few steps from a previous excerpt on how to start your own destiny change.

STEPS TO START YOUR OWN DESTINY CHANGE

1. Start thinking about where you want to go from here

2. Take control of your own time

3. It's okay for you to say No!

4. Determine what is valuable to you

5. Ask yourself what you can learn from this situation and make a difference

6. Create a vision of yourself being at peace after the healing process

7. Write out 5 of your strengths and mediate on them

8. Write out 5 of your weakness and improve on them

9. Schedule a set time just for you and God alone

10. Ask God what areas in your life need to be lined up with Him to move on

Here are 2 scriptures that I meditated on:

Matthew 6:33 – "But seek ye first the kingdom of God, and his righteousness; and all these things shall be added unto you."

Matthew 4:4 - "But he answered and said, it is written, Man shall not live by bread alone, but by every word that proceedeth out of the mouth of God."

Questions to Ponder

- What does forgiveness mean to you?

- What does healing mean to you?

- Where will these thoughts eventually lead me in the end?

- Are these thoughts and emotions spiritually sound?

- Are these thoughts going to build you up or tear you down?

Are You Finally Ready To Write Your Story?

Now is the time for *You* to share *your* story.

It is the time for you to put pen/paper together, or type –write down your thoughts, just as God has already given to you. Just like these bold and courageous women, and these young adults are sharing their truth; it's time for you to break the cycle, break the silence and write your own truth!!!

SPEAK YOUR TRUTH BECAUSE YOUR TRUTH MATTERS!!

So, are you ready to be bold, strong: write, share and publish your truth, so that you will be a blessing to so many, which will encourage others to do the same? Also, I share with you, healing will take place –in so many areas of your life.

If you believe that this is your time, and you are ready to share your story, and you want more information about how you can become a published author, or a published co-author, and you want more information,

EMAIL: <u>Allisongdaniels@verizon.net</u> OR visit: Allisongdaniels.com

Allison G. Daniels

ALLISON G. DANIELS VISIONARY,
EMPOWERED TO WIN BOOK SERIES

BOOKS PUBLISHED BY AGD PUBLISHING SERVICES

www.allisongdaniels.com

Unshakable Faith, 1st Edition Anthology
Allison G. Daniels, Visionary, 2022

Empowered to Win, 3rd Edition Anthology
Allison G. Daniels, Visionary, 2022

Empowered to Win, 2nd Edition Anthology
Allison G. Daniels, Visionary, 2021

Spiritual Mindset
Pastor Daniel T. Mangrum, 2020

Exposing Shame
Co-Pastor Sabrina A. Mangrum, 2020

Pressing Forward
Bishop Mary E. Adams, 2020

Breakthrough: Book of Poems and Prayers
Felicia Edmond, 2020

ALLISON G. DANIELS

The Low Diabetic Scare
1st Children's Book
Shatyna Lee, 2021

ARISE Devotional Book: Arise to the New in Christ
Elder Felicia Edmond, 2022

BOOKS AUTHORED BY VISIONARY, ALLISON G. DANIELS

Women Be Free, Volume 1 (2023)

Unshakable Faith, Volume 1 (2022)

Empowered to Win, 3rd Edition, (2022)

Empowered to Win, 2nd Edition, (2020)

Empowered to Win, 1st Edition, (2019)

Walk in your Authority: Unleash the Divine Power from Within (2016)

Tribute to President Barak Obama (2014)

Love Poems (2014)

How to Self-Publish a Book (2014)

Pink Side of Me (2014)

Life Goes On (2013)

When I Did When My Loved Passed Away (2013)

Quotes of Wisdom (2012)

ALLISON G. DANIELS

Poems for all Occasions (2012)

Happy Valentine's Day with Love (2012)

Daily Words of Wisdom (2012)

The Spirit of a Woman (2011—2012)

A Tribute to Whitney Houston (2012)

A Tribute to President Obama (2010)

Poems for all Occasions (2007)

Comfort Corner (2003)

Changing Winds (2003)

Love Expressed Through a Poet (2003)

Mother I Love You (2003)

Taking Back My Life (2002)

Facing Tomorrow (2000)

I Dream in Colors (1998)

Revitalizing Your Spirit (1998)

A Glimpse of Glory (1998)

Black Man I Love You (1997)

EMPOWERED TO WIN!

Beyond Hope (1996)

Yearning for Love (1996)

Jesus a Joy to Call My Own (1996)

Sweet Memories of Yesterday (1996)

Private Fears That No One Else Hears (1995)

Untold Feelings of a Poet (1993)

CO-AUTHORED BY ALLISON G. DANIELS

Kaleidoscope: Developing an Optimistic View of Life (2022)

Let Go or Be Dragged: Experiencing Freedom from Negativity and Trauma (2022)

From the Heart of a Caregiver: A Little Book Filled with a Lot of Love (2022)

Clinging to the Vine: Stories to Help You Draw Closer to the Lord (2022)

#BeastMode: What Does Success Look Like to You? (2022)

Finally Free, Volume 2, (2022)

Image in the Mirror, II (2022)

Finally Free (2021)

Birthing Your Book (2020)

Speaking My Truth (2019)

Writing is Essential (2019)

Sharing our Prayers (2018)

ALLISON G. DANIELS

Female Architect (2016)

Coaching Guru Book II (2015)

Teenage Girls (2014)

The Female Leader (2014)

Bully Me No More (2013)

Celebration of Life (2013)

How to Survive When Your Ship is Sinking (2012)

Releasing Strongholds (2012)

BOOK COACH/CONSULTANT

ALLISON G. DANIELS

Broken Promises by Kristian Gregory-Lee

I Believe I Can Fly by Jackie Petty

Behind the Chair by Alice (Doll)

Made in the USA
Middletown, DE
30 September 2023

39640847R00126